SCHOLASTIC

Traits Writing™

Student Handbook

Credits

Cover: © Masterfile; p. 39 b: © Robert Gubbins/Shutterstock; p. 47 b: © fotohunter/Shutterstock; 55 b: © Silvia Jansen/iStockphoto; p. 65 b: © Charles D. Winters/Photo Researchers, Inc.; p. 73 b: © Jurisam/iStockphoto; 81 b: © Gbrundin/iStockphoto; p. 91 b: © Dennis MacDonald/Photolibrary; p. 99 b: © Maica/iStockphoto; p. 107 b: © Kati Molin/Shutterstock; p. 117 b: © Masterfile; p. 125 b: © Corbis Bridge/Alamy; p. 133 b: © LilKar/Shutterstock; p. 143 b: © PhotoStock-Israel/Alamy; p. 151 b: © Ron Elmy/age fotostock; p. 159 b: © Gogo Images/Glow Images; p. 169 b: © Konmesa/Shutterstock; p. 177 b: © Nelson Marques/Shutterstock; p. 185 b: © Chris Whitehead/Jupiterimages; p. 195 b: © Peter Wey/Shutterstock; p. 203 b: © Fedor Selivanov/Shutterstock; p. 211 b: © Abigail Pope/Media Bakery

Trait Mates Illustrations: Wook Jin Jung

ISBN-13: 978-0-545-35813-2
ISBN-10: 0-545-35813-2

Contents

Week

1

The Writing Process

Week

2

Prewriting

Week

3

Drafting

Week

4

Revising

Week

5

Editing

Getting Started

The writing process helps you understand how to create a piece of writing. The writing traits give you a common language for discussing and assessing what you create. The traits are

- Ideas
- Organization
- Voice
- Word Choice
- Sentence Fluency
- Conventions
- Presentation

In the weeks to come, you'll learn more about each trait and how to use it as you prewrite, draft, revise, edit, and publish your writing. What makes the traits so great? They help YOU become a great writer!

Steps in the Writing Process

The Writing Process

Prewriting, drafting, revising, editing, and finishing and publishing are steps in the writing process. As you work through these steps, you share your writing with others and strive to improve it. That's where the writing traits come in. The traits help you know what to do at each step of the writing process. As a result, your writing gets stronger and stronger.

The Writing Process

(Prewriting)

- Use prewriting strategies such as brainstorming, talking, and reading to gather information.
- Think about the best way to organize your thoughts.
- Consider your audience and your purpose for writing.

(Drafting)

- Use prewriting ideas to make drafting decisions.
- Let ideas flow, knowing you can revise later.
- Get thoughts down without worrying too much about conventions.
- Begin to structure the body.

(Revising)

- Use accurate and interesting details that reveal your unique perspective on the topic.
- Consider the tone and use a voice that will connect with the reader.
- Start out strong and end just as strong.
- Refine words and sentences so they are precise and varied.

(Editing)

- Check spelling and look up words if needed.
- Punctuate sentences accurately and start paragraphs in the right places.
- Use capital letters correctly.
- Apply standard rules of English grammar.

After editing comes pizza! Didn't your teacher read the manual?!

What I Know About the Writing Process

Match each step in the writing process with its definition and the traits(s) that apply to it. Write the letters in the blanks.

Steps in the Writing Process

A. Prewriting   **B.** Drafting   **C.** Revising
D. Editing   **E.** Finishing/Publishing

Definitions:

1. _____ Use conventions to prepare your writing for the reader.

2. _____ Make changes—cut, add, and move text around.

3. _____ Gather information and plan what you will write.

4. _____ Get your ideas down in rough form.

5. _____ Give your writing a pleasing appearance.

Traits (More than one step may apply to each trait.):

1. _____ Ideas

2. _____ Organization

3. _____ Voice

4. _____ Word Choice

5. _____ Sentence Fluency

6. _____ Conventions

7. _____ Presentation

"Boom, Boom, Ain't It Great to Be Writing?" Lyrics

Add your group's new stanza to "Boom, Boom, Ain't It Great to Be Writing?"

My Group's Trait: _____

Verse:

_____

_____

_____

_____

Chorus:

Boom, boom, ain't it great to be writing?

Boom, boom, ain't it great to be writing?

Working and thinking the whole day through,

Boom, boom, ain't it great to be writing?

Voice lessons, anyone?

Voice

Something Decidedly Different About Me

What is something about you that is different from anyone else you know? Explain it here. Let your guard down. Use words and phrases that will make your piece sound as unique as you are.

Title: _____

_____

_____

_____

_____

_____

_____

_____

_____

_____

_____

_____

_____

_____

_____

My body is a puzzle piece, with eyes above and wheels below. I'd call that "decidedly different."

Sentence Fluency

The ABCs of Writing

Think of a writing-related word that begins with the letter assigned to you. Name a trait or step in the writing process that the word connects to. Then write a sentence containing the word that offers advice to writers.

My Letter: _____

A Writing-Related Word That Begins With My Letter:

_____

Writing Trait or Step in the Writing Process to Which It Connects:

_____

A Sentence Containing the Word (Try to pack in as much useful information to writers as possible!):

_____

_____

_____

_____

_____

_____

_____

_____

Steps in the Writing Process

Prewriting → Drafting → Revising → Editing → Finishing/Publishing

Prewriting

When you prewrite, you choose a topic for writing, identify your purpose and audience, and begin to organize what you will say and how you will say it. Prewriting is essential because it helps you explore your writing possibilities, and gives you a place to begin.

[Think About: **Prewriting**]

☐ Did I make a list, read a book or Web article, write ideas in my journal, draw pictures, observe things around me, listen as a writer, summarize what I know and what I want to know, and/or brainstorm or use a graphic organizer to think about different ideas for writing or focusing my topic?

☐ Did I think through my topic so it is clear and focused?

☐ Did I plan the best way to organize my ideas?

☐ Did I consider the audience for my writing and choose a voice that will speak to it?

Wait just a Trait Mate minute! There's nothing about conventions on this list!

Chill! You'll get your turn, buddy. It's all about ideas for now.

Conventions

Ideas

Prewriting

Prewriting a Poem

Some prewriting techniques:
- Brainstorm ideas with others.
- Make a list of your ideas.
- Use a graphic organizer.
- Freewrite or draw pictures about your topic.
- Observe the world as a writer and keep a journal.
- Summarize what you know and what you want to know.
- Gather information by reading.

Which technique will you use to write a poem about writing?

_____

_____

Use this space for prewriting your poem.

A Writing Treat

Use this sheet to prewrite a recipe for the trait you were assigned. For inspiration, refer to the trait definition, key qualities, and sample passage on the All About . . . sheet.

Trait: _____

Recipe Ingredients

- _____

- _____

- _____

- _____

- _____

- _____

- _____

Recipe Directions

_____

_____

_____

_____

_____

_____

_____

_____

Prewriting

What Should I Write About?

List some ideas for writing, inspired by events from your own life or books and articles you have read.

1. _____

   _____

2. _____

   _____

3. _____

   _____

4. _____

   _____

5. _____

   _____

6. _____

   _____

Circle the idea you find most interesting and then choose the mode in which you'll write about it.

      Narrative: to tell a story

      Expository: to inform or explain

      Persuasive: to construct an argument

Develop your idea using a prewriting technique discussed earlier in the week.

Create a Video

Create a video that gives younger students tips on prewriting. Use the chart below to plan your video. Under "Audio," write what the audience will hear in each part. Under "Visual," write what the audience will see.

Audio	Visual

When your plan is complete, write a short script and prepare your visuals.

Steps in the Writing Process

Prewriting → Drafting → Revising → Editing → Finishing/Publishing

Drafting

When you prewrite, you come up with a topic for a piece, and begin to think about organization and voice. When you draft, you fine-tune your thinking even further by considering why you're writing the piece and who will read it. You might think about your lead, your ending, and details to include in the body. Got it? A rough draft should be just that—rough. You'll polish the piece when you revise. For now, you just need to get the piece moving.

[Think About: **Drafting**]

☐ Did I refer to my prewriting ideas before starting to write?

☐ Did I let my ideas flow, knowing that I can add, cut, or change anything I want to later?

☐ Did I think about what the reader might want or need to know about my topic?

☐ Am I moving toward a strong beginning, middle, and end in a way that is easy to follow?

☐ Did I get my ideas down without worrying too much about spelling, punctuation, capitalization, and grammar?

I'm cold. Is there a draft in here?

Lots of 'em—but not that kind.

Welcome to this book's first bad joke of many.

Organization

Voice

Word Choice

Drafting

My Take on Drafting

(Part 1)

Authors know themselves as writers and what motivates them to start drafting. What motivates you to start drafting? On the lines below, write your thoughts.

_____

_____

_____

_____

(Part 2)

Now, read the draft of your beginning-of-year benchmark paper and assess it, using the Student-Friendly Scoring Guides on pages 232–236. Circle a trait you're handling well.

Ideas   Organization   Voice
        Word Choice   Sentence Fluency

On the lines below, copy a passage from your draft that gives evidence that you're handling that trait well.

_____

_____

_____

_____

_____

_____

My Blog About Writing

Draft a blog entry that is a progress report on your beginning-of-year benchmark paper. You might use the following questions to help you come up with ideas:

- What have I accomplished so far?
- What prewriting techniques did I use before drafting?
- Which traits are strong in my writing? Which are not?
- What is my plan for the paper? What will I do next?

A Writer's Blog by _____

(name)

Today's Date: _____

_____

_____

_____

_____

_____

_____

_____

_____

_____

_____

A Summer Tale

Draft the opening paragraph of a story that takes place in summer in your neighborhood. Begin by giving your story a title, and identifying the main character(s) and setting.

Story Title: _____

Main Character(s): _____

_____

Setting (time and place): _____

_____

Now draft your opening paragraph. Write your story in the first person, as Walter Dean Myers does in *Harlem Summer*— and give it a distinctive voice.

_____

_____

_____

_____

_____

_____

_____

_____

_____

An Extreme First Draft

With a partner, reread the passage from Walter Dean Myers's *Harlem Summer*. Discuss what you like about it and what Myers does especially well as a writer.

Now work backward by imagining you are Walter Dean Myers, writing a first draft of the passage. In the space below, write that rough version, with none of the elements that make the final version work so well—just-right words, juicy details, strong voice, and so on.

_____

_____

_____

_____

_____

_____

_____

_____

_____

_____

_____

_____

_____

Steps in the Writing Process

Prewriting

Drafting

Revising

Editing

Finishing/
Publishing

Revising

You discover what you want to say when you prewrite and get your ideas down on paper when you draft. From there, you revise. You add, delete, reword, and rearrange material to make your writing strong and clear. Revising can be challenging, but the traits make it easier by giving you something concrete to think about. Even the most accomplished writers revise. Once the piece says exactly what they want it to say, they move on to editing.

[Think About: **Revising**]

☐ Did I focus the topic and use accurate and original details to elaborate on the main idea?

☐ Do all the parts of the piece fit together logically from beginning to end?

☐ Did I add energy to the piece by expressing how I think and feel about the topic?

☐ Are my words and sentences precise, fresh, and varied?

Imagine an Alien

Think about how author PJ Haarsma comes up with his aliens for The Softwire series. Then work with your group to elaborate on the following sentence:

I am an alien.

What do I look like? Add one physical feature of the alien by making a comparison to a familiar person or animal, such as, "My eyes bug out like a fly's at a picnic."

_____

_____

How do I act? Add a behavior of the alien by making a comparison to a familiar person or animal.

_____

_____

What can I do? Add a unique ability the alien has, inspired by a familiar person or animal.

_____

_____

Where can you find me? Add a setting for the alien, inspired by a place you know.

_____

_____

Use this information to write a clear description of your alien, on a separate sheet of paper.

If You Want to Revise for . . .

Think about the revision techniques for Ideas, Organization, Voice, Word Choice, and Sentence Fluency.

Take an index card with a trait name on it. Then review the Revision Techniques sheet and, below, write down two techniques that relate to your trait. After that, write down your own revision technique.

Techniques to revise for _____

1. _____

   _____

2. _____

   _____

My own technique: _____

_____

_____

When you finish, find a classmate with a different trait, swap handbooks, read what he or she wrote, and place your initials next to his or her trait, below. Keep swapping until you've read revision techniques for all five traits.

Ideas _____   **Organization** _____   **Voice** _____

Word Choice _____   **Sentence Fluency** _____

The Museum of My Life

Imagine yourself 50 years from now. A museum has been built in your honor, and you've been asked to give the opening address. How would you begin?

To prepare the introduction of your address, answer the three questions David Harrison asked himself when he was preparing his address for the school named in his honor.

1. What should I talk about?

_____

_____

_____

2. Who will my audience be?

_____

_____

_____

3. How should I say what I want to say?

_____

_____

_____

Now try this:

Draft your introduction on a separate sheet of paper. Read the piece aloud to a few classmates. Ask for feedback and revise accordingly.

Say What?

Reread David Harrison's all-time worst sentence. Revise it—shorten it, clarify it, make it flow. Then, write an all-time worst sentence of your own. Use a separate sheet if needed.

Peter was a rabbit, had always known, though at times it wasn't easy when his siblings taunted him and called him "Poor Reception" because as a twitchy-nosed, witless bunny he scampered into the mower's path and forfeited both ears, for in those days you couldn't get decent reception on your TV for the Mary Tyler Moore Show or Sid Caesar either if you didn't have a wire antenna called rabbit ears perched on top and, of course, Peter had neither, but even so he knew he was a rabbit as sure as carrots are orange, only not that icky sort of orange you get in off-brand sodas or two-day-old road-kill on July 24th, which always queasied Peter's stomach and made his lettuce taste like spinach left out so long it forms that slick kind of green goop, and certainly not the edgy orange of an ambitious sun auditioning for the role of sunset in an Angelina Jolie movie, which, really, when he thought about it, was more of a reddish-purple than orange, but a rabbit was he and proud of it.

My revision:

_____

_____

_____

_____

My own all-time worst sentence:

_____

_____

_____

_____

Steps in the Writing Process

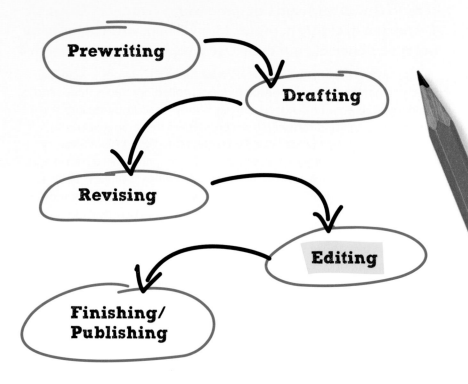

Prewriting → Drafting → Revising → Editing → Finishing/Publishing

Editing

After you prewrite, draft, and revise your piece, it's time to edit it, or clean it up for the reader. This is an important step in the writing process because in order for the reader to understand what you have to say, he or she can't be confused by errors in spelling, punctuation, paragraphing, capitalization, or grammar and usage. When you edit, you apply rules of standard English to make sure your piece is a breeze to read and easy to understand.

[Think About: **Editing**]

- Did I check my spelling against a print or electronic resource and, if necessary, correct any misspelled words?

- Did I use punctuation accurately and effectively to make my ideas flow?

- Did I start paragraphs in the right places?

- Did I capitalize words correctly?

- Did I follow the rules of standard English grammar and usage? Or did I break them for stylistic reasons?

I'll take spelling and punctuation on whole wheat, with mustard, please.

Uh, you're not building a sandwich. You're building a great piece of writing!

Yeah, but writing makes me hungry.

Conventions

Presentation

Editing

Punctuation Power

Here's your chance to try out Patricia T. O'Conner's techniques from *Words Fail Me*.

1. Write two separate but related simple sentences. Then combine them into a compound sentence using a comma and the word *and* or *but*.

   My Two Simple Sentences:

   _____

   _____

   _____

   My Compound Sentence:

   _____

   _____

2. Write a sentence in which you set off ideas with dashes and/or parentheses.

   _____

   _____

3. Write a sentence that ends with an exclamation point. Then, write a sentence on the same topic that conveys excitement—without requiring an exclamation point.

   Sentence 1:

   _____

   _____

   Sentence 2:

   _____

   _____

My "No Excuses" List

List five conventions rules that you will follow every time you write—no excuses!

1. _____

_____

_____

2. _____

_____

_____

3. _____

_____

_____

4. _____

_____

_____

5. _____

_____

_____

Check your writing against this list whenever you're taking it to completion. You are the editor!

Editing

Caption Challenge

Choose four animal photographs. Then describe each one below and write a caption for it. See how many different punctuation marks you can use to make your captions interesting and informative.

1. Photo description: _____

   _____

   Caption: _____

   _____

2. Photo description: _____

   _____

   Caption: _____

   _____

3. Photo description: _____

   _____

   Caption: _____

   _____

4. Photo description: _____

   _____

   Caption: _____

   _____

What's Your Story?

Work with a partner to brainstorm ideas for your short story.

Genre:

__ historical fiction   __ sci-fi   __ mystery __ adventure

__ realistic fiction   __ fantasy   __ humor   __ steampunk

__ folktale, fairy tale, or fable __ tall tale   __ horror   __ cyberpunk

__ romance   __ crime/thriller   __ dystopia __ Western

Setting (time and place):

_____

_____

Main characters and what readers will learn about them:

_____

_____

_____

Plot (What happens? What is the conflict? How is it resolved?):

_____

_____

_____

Theme: courage (How will you work in this theme? Through character actions? From a plot idea? In some other way?)

_____

_____

_____

Editing

Editing Marks

Mark	Meaning	Example
℘	Delete material.	The writing is ~~so~~ good.
sp	Correct the spelling or spell it out.	We are exploring ②(sp) traits this (weak)(sp). → week
◡	Close space.	To day is publishing day.
∧	Insert a letter, word, or phrase.	My teacher has ∧ books. → wonderful
℘	Change a letter.	She is a great wr⍟ter. → i
#	Add a space.	Don't forget a#strong lead.
∿	Transpose letters or words.	She ra⍟ed the piece with flair!
≡	Change to a capital letter.	We have j. k. Rowling to thank for Harry Potter's magic.
/	Change to a lowercase letter.	"A Writer's work is never Done" was his favorite saying.
¶	Start a new paragraph.	"What day is it?" he inquired. ¶"It's National Writing Day," she replied.
⊙	Add a period.	Think about all the traits as you write ⊙

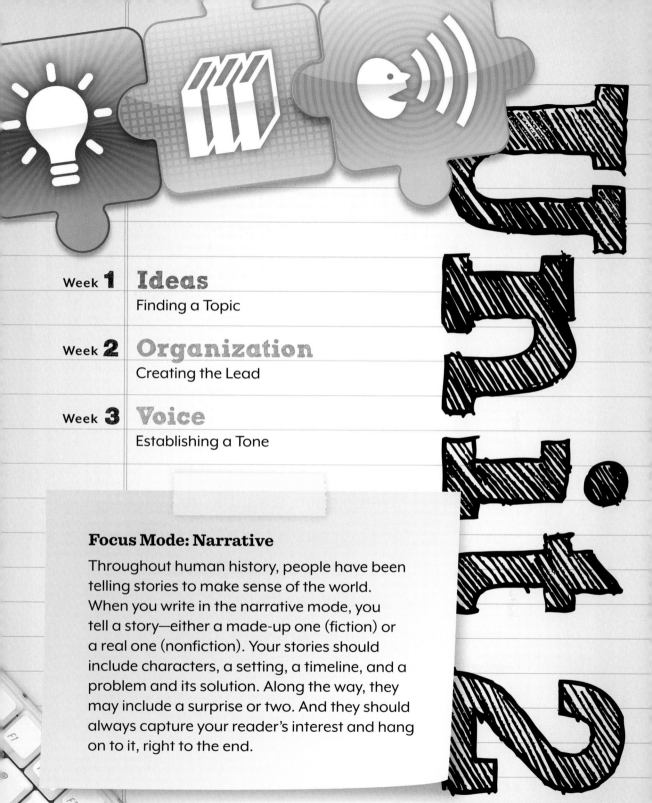

Focus Mode: Narrative

Throughout human history, people have been telling stories to make sense of the world. When you write in the narrative mode, you tell a story—either a made-up one (fiction) or a real one (nonfiction). Your stories should include characters, a setting, a timeline, and a problem and its solution. Along the way, they may include a surprise or two. And they should always capture your reader's interest and hang on to it, right to the end.

- **Finding a Topic** ⋯⋯⋯⋯
- Focusing the Topic
- Developing the Topic
- Using Details

Focus Mode: Narrative
Theme: Courage

Ideas

Ideas are your central message—the main thoughts you want to share. To make your ideas strong, choose a topic you care about and focus on one interesting aspect of it. From there, weave in original and unexpected details to open your readers' eyes and show them something they might otherwise overlook.

Never settle for anything less than a 24-karat topic.

Finding a Topic

Topics for writing are all around you—in what you see, hear, experience, and daydream about every day. When you find the perfect topic, your mind races with exciting possibilities. Your main objective should be to offer a clear, central theme or simple, original story line—something unique, important, meaningful, and memorable.

Ideas

How is panning for gold like finding a good topic for writing?

Mining for Ideas

You can get ideas for your narrative writing from many sources. Here are four places to start.

1. Life Experiences

We've all experienced times of failure and success, taken a stand on something we believe is important, or faced up to a fear.

What life experience could you write about?

_____

_____

2. Newspaper and Magazine Articles

Where else can you read about acts of heroism, people who survived natural disasters, or an unbelievable win by your favorite sports team?

What recent headline do you think could inspire a great story?

_____

_____

3. The Arts: Music, Painting, Photography, Dance, Drama

The rich details in photographs and paintings can provide writers with ideas for the setting, characters, and plot of a story.

What kind of art would you turn to for a story idea?

_____

_____

4. Television Shows, Movies, Books

Everyone has a favorite TV show, movie, or book. Writers are often inspired by their favorite characters, plots, or settings.

What TV show, movie, or book has inspired you to write a story?

_____

_____

R.A.F.T.S. 1

You are one of fifteen miners rescued after spending two weeks trapped underground because an explosion blocked your path to the surface. While waiting to be rescued, you kept a journal of your experience. You've been asked to share with your local newspaper a journal entry that tells the story of your struggle to survive. Pick one day and tell everything that happened, from morning to night. Pay attention to choosing a topic for your entry that is not too broad.

Role: miner
Audience: newspaper readers
Format: journal entry
Topic: surviving a mine accident
Strong Verbs: share, tell

Write your journal entry on a separate sheet of paper. Before you begin to write, jot down some details you might include.

Think About

- Have I chosen a topic that I really like?
- Do I have something new to say about this topic?
- Am I writing about what I know and care about?
- Have I gathered enough information about it so that I'm ready to write?

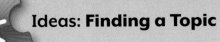

Jump Start Sheet

Unit Project Topic: _____

Days 1 and 3: My Unit Project To-Do List

- _____

- _____

- _____

- _____

Day 5: My Six-Word Statement on Courage

_____ _____ _____ _____ _____ _____

Focus on Grammar and Usage

Search your writing for two sentences that would benefit from the use of interjections. Rewrite them here, with interjections.

1. _____

    _____

    _____

2. _____

    _____

    _____

Write-On Sheet

Ideas: Finding a Topic

Preview

A Film Reviewer

In the space below, capture your thoughts about the job
of a film reviewer.

1. What does the title "film reviewer" make you think of? Do you
   have any questions about the job? Write them here.

   _____

   _____

   _____

   _____

2. Film reviewers see and think about lots of films. What about their
   job do you think would be most interesting? Most difficult?

   _____

   _____

   _____

   _____

3. Have you ever been inspired to see a movie—or totally turned off
   from one—by reviews you read or heard about?

   _____

   _____

   _____

   _____

Bonus: Use the Internet to discover more about a film reviewer's job.
Write your findings on note cards and share them with classmates.

What's the Story?

Imagine you're going to write a review of the film version of a favorite novel or short story. Fill in key information about the film and then write the narrative summary portion of your review.

Film's Title: _____

Main Character: _____

Secondary Characters: _____

_____

When and where the story takes place: _____

_____

Conflict the main character faces and how it is resolved:

_____

_____

_____

My Narrative Summary: _____

_____

_____

_____

_____

_____

_____

_____

_____

Ideas

The movie was so-so, but the popcorn was excellent!

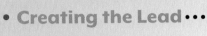

- **Creating the Lead** ⋯⋯⋯⋯⋯⋯
- Using Sequence Words and Transition Words
- Structuring the Body
- Ending With a Sense of Resolution

Focus Mode: Narrative
Theme: Courage

Organization

Organization is about how your idea unfolds from beginning to end—how you structure and arrange your details. An organized piece of writing begins engagingly, moves along logically, and ends satisfyingly. You give readers the right amount of information at the right moments. When your organization is working, following the idea is effortless.

Hey writers, make like the sun. Rise and SHINE!

Creating the Lead

You get one chance to make a good first impression with a piece of writing—and that is with your lead. Whether it's a fact, question, or quotation, a good lead introduces your topic to readers and assures them that you have a plan and a direction. It entices readers by providing a lively, tantalizing glimpse of what is to come.

Organization

How is a great lead that draws the reader into a story like a beautiful sunrise that marks a new day?

How to Hook a Reader

These five types of leads are proven winners for grabbing the reader's attention right from the start.

1. Analogy

What it does: uses two items that share an obvious relationship (flies + garbage) to highlight a similar, less obvious relationship between a different set of ideas (bad luck + me)

Example: Bad luck usually stuck to me like flies to garbage.

2. Metaphor

What it does: illustrates a word or idea by equating it with something seemingly unrelated (Aida + statue)

Example: Aida was a statue, cool, calm, and silently still. "If you don't bother them, they won't bother you," she told herself. She only hoped the colossal grizzly in front of her felt the same way.

3. Description

What it does: explains the setting, characters, or events

Example: I live in Omaha, Nebraska, land of prairies and cattle. I grew up on a ranch, famous for black Angus. Never met an Angus cow? Let me introduce you to Hairy.

4. Surprising Fact

What it does: offers information that the reader doesn't expect

Example: By the time you are 14 years old, your body will have replaced its entire skeleton twice.

5. Scenario

What it does: crystallizes what will be covered

Example: Jack woke up, expecting it to be like every other day. Little did he know that his life was about to change—forever.

R.A.F.T.S. 2

You are editor of a nature magazine called *The World's Coolest Animals!* As editor, you write a short "letter from the editor" to introduce each issue. Your next issue features articles on surprising encounters between people and wild animals. In your letter you need to tell the funniest or scariest story of a wild animal encounter that you've ever heard. It should grab readers' attention right from the start and make them want to keep reading.

Role: editor of a nature magazine
Audience: magazine readers
Format: letter from the editor
Topic: a funny or scary encounter with a wild animal
Strong Verbs: tell, grab

Write your letter on a separate sheet of paper. Before you begin to write, jot down some details you might include.

Think About

- Did I give the reader something interesting to think about right from the start?
- Will the reader want to keep reading?
- Have I tried to get the reader's attention?
- Did I let the reader know what is coming?

Jump Start Sheet

Unit Project Topic: _____

Days 1 and 3: My Unit Project To-Do List

- _____
- _____
- _____
- _____

Day 5: My Six-Word Statement on Courage

_____ _____ _____ _____ _____ _____

Focus on Word Study

Root: *audi*

Meaning: _____

Common Words That Contain the Root:

1.

2.

3.

My Wacky Word

_____

_____

_____

_____

Write-On Sheet

Preview

Sharon Draper, author of

Little Sister Is Not My Name!

Answer the questions below. Discuss the answers with a partner.

1. **Sharon Draper taught English for 30 years. How do you think this experience helps her create stories for young people?**

   _____

   _____

   _____

   _____

2. **Draper's character, Sassy, doesn't like being the youngest member of her family. Where do you think Draper might have gotten this idea for a character?**

   _____

   _____

   _____

   _____

3. **Which book in the Sassy series looks most interesting:** *Little Sister Is Not My Name!, The Birthday Storm, The Silver Secret,* **or** *The Dazzle Disaster Dinner Party?* **Why did its title capture your attention?**

   _____

   _____

   _____

   _____

A Sassy Start

Use this chart to evaluate and compare the lead from *Little Sister Is Not My Name!* and another piece of narrative writing.

Starting a piece of writing is like starting a jigsaw puzzle. Ooh... Ooh... pick me!

Little Sister Is Not My Name!	Your Choice: _____
Type of Lead:	
_____	_____

How the lead . . .

- introduces characters

_____ _____

_____ _____

- describes the setting

_____ _____

_____ _____

- presents a conflict or problem

_____ _____

_____ _____

Did the author grab your attention? Why or why not?

_____ _____

_____ _____

This lead could have been stronger if:

_____ _____

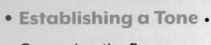

- **Establishing a Tone** ⋯⋯⋯⋯⋯
- Conveying the Purpose
- Creating a Connection to the Audience
- Taking Risks to Create Voice

Focus Mode: Narrative
Theme: Courage

Voice

Voice is the energy and attitude of a piece of writing. In fiction, voice can take on almost any tone, from humorous or hopeful to serious or somber. In nonfiction, it is often compelling, authoritative, and knowledgeable. You arrive at the right voice for a piece by thinking deeply about your purpose and audience for it. You "speak" in a way that connects to your audience.

Lose the laryngitis. Find your voice!

Establishing a Tone

When you speak, you use your tone of voice to help express how you feel. The same is true for writing. When you establish a tone that is compelling and right for the piece, readers feel your conviction. They want to keep reading because they feel you're speaking directly to them. Multiple tones can be present in a single piece; it's the sum of the tones that creates voice.

A gong has a very distinctive tone—and so should your writing. Why?

Voice: **Establishing a Tone**

Top 10 Tones

How you think and feel about your topic should come through in your tone. Here are ten tones that you might want to bring to your writing.

1. silly

"A whizzpopper!" cried the BFG, beaming at her. "Us giants is making whizzpoppers all the time! Whizzpopping is a sign of happiness . . ."

—Roald Dahl, *The BFG*

2. sincere

[It] slavishly follows every rule of the kids' fantasy franchise genre, but it's a well-executed and imagined world.

—Helen O'Hara, Empire Movie Review: *Percy Jackson and the Lightning Thief*

3. nostalgic

Wilbur never forgot Charlotte. Although he loved her children and grandchildren dearly, none of the new spiders ever . . . took her place in his heart.

—E. B. White, *Charlotte's Web*

4. friendly

Chewing on the end of my pencil, I got back to my list, which Gram said was one of the things I did best. I had all kinds of lists in my notebook, the shortest being "Things I am Good At" which consisted of 1) Soap Carving, 2) Worrying, and 3) Making Lists.

—Pam Muñoz Ryan, *Becoming Naomi León*

5. passionate

Ronald stared at the line of shapes he longed to know how to read; they seemed to him as magical as fairy-tale pictures in his book. Words and trees—and knights and dragons—were what Ronald wanted.

—Anne E. Neimark, *Myth Maker: J. R. R. Tolkien*

6. sarcastic

Yep, so that means I was staring at a geometry book that was at least thirty years older than I was. I couldn't believe it. How horrible was that?

—Sherman Alexie, *The Absolutely True Diary of a Part-Time Indian*

7. stubborn

Cookie was not like other dogs. She was easily the most strong-willed person—and I mean person—I had ever met.

—Gary Paulsen, *Puppies, Dogs, and Blue Northers*

8. anxious

This kind of thing only happens in the movies. Not to real people like us. Here we are—stuck in a dingy elevator with dim lights. This can't be happening.

—Sharon Draper, *Sassy*

9. resigned

This was one of those tragedies that needed a family that knew what it was doing. Like the Kennedys or the Queen of England and her bunch. Not a family like ours that comes unglued if someone doesn't follow the morning bathroom schedule.

—Barbara Park, *Mick Harte Was Here*

10. frightened

As it got closer, Chet could see the dark shape of an enormous fish, bigger than him. Even bigger than Uncle Jerry. Two black eyes peered up through the water. Chet's heart stopped.

—Lauren Tarshis, *I Survived . . .*

R.A.F.T.S. 3

You are a greeting card writer. Your next assignment is to create two one-paragraph birthday cards with contrasting tones, such as silly and serious or sarcastic and sentimental. Design your cards so that they will fly off the shelves and bring smiles to recipients' faces. Be sure to pay close attention to establishing opposing tones.

Role: greeting card writer
Audience: people celebrating birthdays
Format: birthday card
Topic: cards with opposing tones
Strong Verbs: create, design

Write your birthday cards on separate sheets of paper. Before you begin to write, jot down some details you might include.

Think About

- Can I name the primary tone of my writing? (for example, happy, frustrated, knowledgeable, scared, convincing)
- Have I varied the tone from the beginning to the end?
- Have I been expressive?
- Did I show that I care about this topic?

Jump Start Sheet

Days 1 and 3: My Unit Project To-Do List

- _____
- _____
- _____
- _____

Day 5: My Six-Word Statement on Courage

_____ _____ _____ _____ _____ _____

Focus on Grammar and Usage

Write one sentence with a compound subject, one sentence with a compound predicate, and one sentence with *both* a compound subject and a compound predicate.

1. _____

   _____

2. _____

   _____

3. _____

   _____

   _____

Write-On Sheet

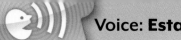

Preview

Lauren Tarshis, author of
I Survived the Shark Attacks of 1916

Answer the questions below and discuss them with a partner.

1. Lauren Tarshis is the editor of *StoryWorks*, a kids' magazine that features fiction and nonfiction writing by some of the world's best children's authors. Do you think this affects her writing? How so?

   _____

   _____

   _____

2. The I Survived series includes fictional accounts based on real-life disasters. Other titles in the series include *I Survived Hurricane Katrina, 2005* and *I Survived the Sinking of the Titanic, 1912.* If you were the author, what would the topic of your next book be? Why?

   _____

   _____

   _____

3. How do you think historical fiction writers do their research? How do they find information? What sources do they rely on?

   _____

   _____

   _____

Bonus: On the Internet, find out what a magazine editor does. Write your findings on note cards and share them with the class.

Tons of Tones

On the left, write excerpts from your partner's story. On the right, describe each one's tone.

Story Title: _____

You'd think the Voice mate would have a mouth, right? Who's in charge here?!

Voice

Story Excerpt	Tone

Narrative Publishing Checklist

Think you are ready to go public with your narrative unit project? Use this form to make sure you've covered all the writing bases.

I remembered to

☐ present a clear, well-developed story line.

☐ include fascinating characters that grow and change over time.

☐ convey a time and setting that make sense for the story.

☐ entertain, surprise, and challenge the reader.

☐ develop the story chronologically or take a risk to try a structure that also helps the reader follow the story easily.

☐ use an active voice to engage the reader.

☐ choose words that fit the characters, time, and place.

☐ read my piece aloud to check for places where I should speed up or slow down.

☐ proofread my piece carefully and clean up problems with conventions.

The purpose of my piece is

_____

My favorite part is

_____

What I hope readers will find most memorable about my piece is

_____

Come on. Don't just check all the boxes. There must be something left to do on your project!

Presentation

Focus Mode: Expository

The world is rich with interesting ideas to explore in writing. When you write in the expository mode, you give information about or explain a topic that fascinates you. Think about including captivating details, intriguing insights, and significant life experiences. The best expository writing has a strong, confident voice—a voice that tells the reader you know what you're talking about.

- **Applying Strong Verbs** ································
- Selecting Striking Words and Phrases
- Using Specific and Accurate Words
- Choosing Words That Deepen Meaning

Focus Mode: Expository
Theme: Humor

Word Choice

Words are the building blocks of writing. Well-chosen words bring your ideas into focus. They create images, spark the imagination, and grab the reader's attention. Word choice is verbal alchemy; it's how writers transform the ordinary into the extraordinary. Choose words that move, enlighten, and inspire.

I hear that Voice Mate is a terrible gossip. Just sayin' ...

Word Choice

Applying Strong Verbs

You can "talk"—or you can "discuss," "chatter," or "gossip." Strong verbs deliver the power and punch that brings your writing to life. They capture action precisely in just one little word. When you use strong verbs, your writing is electrifying. It bursts with energy!

What do strong verbs have in common with precious gems?

Word Choice: **Applying Strong Verbs**

It's All About the Action

Here are some techniques for choosing and using strong verbs.

1. Choose dynamic verbs whenever possible.

Choose verbs that describe specific feelings or actions.
Ask yourself: *What feeling or action am I trying to communicate?*
What verb communicates it in a powerful way?

> **Weak:** My legs *were sore* after the three-hour hike.

> **Stronger:** My legs *throbbed* after the three-hour hike.

2. Stretch for uncommon verbs.

Do you often use general verbs such as *walk* or *said*? Substitute specific verbs. A thesaurus can help you find the perfect alternative.

> **Weak:** She *came* into the classroom with her friends.

> **Stronger:** She *sauntered* into the classroom with her friends.

3. Use verbs that don't require adverbs.

Do you often use adverbs to give your writing punch and pizzazz?
Try using more descriptive verbs that don't need adverbs.

> **Weak:** He *really enjoyed* every bite of the cherry pie.

> **Stronger:** He *savored* every bite of the cherry pie.

4. Limit your use of forms of *to be*: *is, am, are, was, were, be, being,* and *been.*

If you want to energize your writing, use one strong verb instead of a verb phrase that includes a form of *to be*.

> **Weak:** The poem "Jabberwocky" *was written* by Lewis Carroll.

> **Stronger:** Lewis Carroll *composed* the poem "Jabberwocky."

R.A.F.T.S. 4

You are the entertainment editor for a local newspaper. Things were rather boring in your hometown until the new water park, LightWaves, opened. Every day throngs of people—adults and children—have been flocking to it and saying the same thing: incredible! Describe the park in a short article announcing to local residents how it will spice up their everyday lives. Use splashy verbs!

Role: entertainment editor
Audience: local residents
Format: short article
Topic: new water park, LightWaves
Strong Verbs: announce, describe

Write your short article on a separate sheet of paper. Before you begin to write, jot down here some details you might include:

Think About

- Have I used action words?
- Did I stretch to get a better word—*scurry* rather than *run*?
- Do my verbs give my writing punch and pizzazz?
- Did I avoid *is, am, are, was, were, be, being,* and *been* whenever I could?

Jump Start Sheet

Unit Project Topic: _____

Days 1 and 3: My Unit Project To-Do List

- _____

- _____

- _____

- _____

Day 5: My Six-Word Statement on Humor

_____ _____ _____ _____ _____ _____

Focus on Word Study

Root: *auto*

Meaning: _____

Common Words That Contain the Root:

1.

2.

3.

My Wacky Word

_____

_____

_____

_____

Write-On Sheet

Word Choice: **Applying Strong Verbs**

A Communications Director

Answer the questions below, on your own or with a partner.

1. From billboards to classroom doors, signs are used for communication. Which sign has caught your eye? Why do you like it?

_____

_____

_____

_____

2. Signs provide information, identification, and advertisement. If you wrote signs for a living, what kind would they be?

_____

_____

_____

_____

3. Pick a favorite radio station, product, store, or sports team. On the lines below, write a three- to six-word idea for a sign or slogan.

_____

_____

_____

_____

Bonus: Look up on the Internet what a communications director does. Write your findings on note cards and share them with a classmate.

Getting Your Message Across

My sign says, "Obey All Traits."

Answer the questions below to help you plan a humorous sign that tells classmates how to behave in a particular situation.

1. Where will your sign be posted?

_____

_____

_____

2. What is the overall message of your sign? What do you want readers to learn or appreciate?

_____

_____

_____

3. What are some strong verbs that you can use in your sign?

_____   _____   _____

_____   _____   _____

_____   _____   _____

4. How will your sign begin? Create a short opening.

_____

_____

_____

- **Crafting Well-Built Sentences**· · · · · · · · ·
- Varying Sentence Types
- Capturing Smooth and Rhythmic Flow
- Breaking the "Rules" to Create Fluency

Focus Mode: Expository
Theme: Humor

Sentence Fluency

Writing may seem like a silent act, but it isn't. When you read your drafts, listen for passages that sound smooth and rhythmic . . . and passages that don't. From there, revise. By doing that, you'll create sentence fluency—the music of language that makes your writing sound as good as it looks.

Stop the clock! I dropped a contact lens in there!

Crafting Well-Built Sentences

You should craft your sentences as carefully as a clock maker assembles a clock. That means writing sentences that are not all short or all long—and that start with different words, not the same word over and over again. Well-built sentences move the reader through the piece.

What do well-built sentences have in common with the gears inside a clock?

Spotlight on Sentences

Here are some techniques that can help you craft well-built sentences.

1. Vary sentence beginnings.

Try This: Maximize the impact of your writing by beginning sentences with different words.

He straightened his goggles. He yelled, "Hike!" He held on as the dogs took off down the trail.

The musher straightened his goggles. "Hike," he yelled. The dogs blasted down the trail.

2. Vary sentence lengths.

Try This: Add rhythm and fluency to your writing by using long and short sentences. Count the words!

People often ask me if I have always been interested in pursuing dangerous and unusual adventures. (16) My answer is, "yes." (4)

3. Watch your grammar.

Try This: Apply standard grammar unless you are purposely bending the rules to add impact.

You can find Internet service almost anywhere today. That is an amazing thing.

You can find Internet service almost anywhere today. Amazing!

4. Connect sentences or sentence parts with conjunctions.

Try This: Use conjunctions *and, but, or, for, nor,* and *yet* to join two shorter, simple sentences into a compound sentence.

We blasted into the library. The librarian looked up. He seemed perturbed. We lowered our voices.

We blasted into the library, and the librarian looked up. He seemed perturbed, so we lowered our voices.

R.A.F.T.S. 5

You're in charge of marketing new books at a publishing company. Writing the online catalog blurb for a new autobiography by Lulu Fontaine, a famous comedienne, is your latest assignment. As any good marketing manager knows, your blurb must not only summarize the book and be informative, but it must also capture the book's spirit—which means it has to be funny. Be sure to use strong, varied sentences.

Role: marketing manager for a book publishing company
Audience: online customers
Format: catalog blurb for a book
Topic: the autobiography of a famous comedienne
Strong Verbs: summarize, capture

Write your blurb on a separate sheet of paper. Before you begin to write, jot down some details you might include.

Think About

- Do my sentences begin in different ways?
- Are my sentences of different lengths?
- Are my sentences grammatically correct unless constructed creatively for impact?
- Have I used conjunctions such as *and, but,* and *or* to connect parts of sentences?

Jump Start Sheet

Days 1 and 3: My Unit Project To-Do List

☐ _____

☐ _____

☐ _____

☐ _____

Day 5: My Six-Word Statement on Humor

_____ _____ _____ _____ _____ _____

Focus on Grammar and Usage

Review your writing, find sentences in which you've used predicate adjectives incorrectly, and revise two of those sentences here.

1. _____

_____

2. _____

_____

Write-On Sheet

Sentence Fluency: **Crafting Well-Built Sentences**

Preview

Megan E. Bryant, author of *Oh My Gods!*

Answer the questions below. Discuss your answers with a partner.

1. Megan E. Bryant is a prolific writer who has produced many books. What would you ask her about her writing habits?

_____

_____

_____

2. *Oh My Gods!* is part of a series about Greek mythology, called Mythlopedia. Why do you think readers are so interested in mythology?

_____

_____

_____

3. The Mythlopedia books about Greek mythology are both informative and humorous. Why would a writer use a humorous voice for a serious topic like Greek mythology?

_____

_____

4. What do you think a writer has to keep in mind in order to make a serious topic into something humorous?

_____

_____

Sentence Analyzer

Use this chart to analyze the sentences in your section from Megan E. Bryant's work.

I'm always being analyzed— and punctuated. It's exhausting!

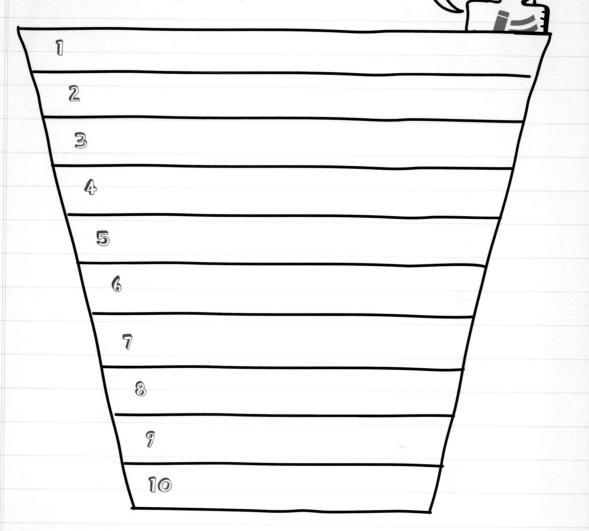

1

2

3

4

5

6

7

8

9

10

Number of sentences in the passage: _____

What do you notice? Are any of the sentences the same length?

_____

Circle the beginnings. Are they the same or different?

_____

- Finding a Topic
- **Focusing the Topic** ....
- Developing the Topic
- Using Details

Focus Mode: Expository
Theme: Humor

Ideas

Ideas are your central message—
the main thoughts you want to share.
To make your ideas strong, choose a
topic you care about and focus on one
interesting aspect of it. From there,
weave in original and unexpected
details to open your readers' eyes
and show them something they might
otherwise overlook.

Focusing the Topic

Focusing a topic is like merging onto a freeway. There are many ideas to choose from, just as there are many lanes to choose from. But sticking to one lane allows you to take passengers where you want them to go in the same way that focusing your topic allows you to take readers where you want them to go. You can relax knowing they won't get lost.

A fresh-squeezed topic is an important part of a well-balanced project.

Ideas

How is squeezing an orange like focusing a writing topic?

Zeroing In on a Topic

After you've selected a topic, it's important to focus it. Here are some tips for doing that.

1. **You've identified a big idea. Now zero in on a small part of it.**

   Ask yourself: What specific aspect of the general topic interests me? What is one small part of the topic I can write about?

2. **Sum up your specific idea in one sentence.**

   Ask yourself: What is the most important thing that I can say about my idea? How can I state it in one sentence?

   Benjamin Franklin, a great American statesman, was known for his dry and clever humor.

3. **Choose information that supports your idea.**

   Ask yourself: What kind of information will help me express my idea?

   I want to capture just how clever Benjamin Franklin was, so I'll quote some of his witty sayings in my paper.

4. **Consider what the reader will need and want to know.**

   Ask yourself: What important facts will the reader need to know to understand my idea?

   Franklin used humor to examine the social issues of his day.
   Comedians today still imitate Franklin's wry, folksy style.

R.A.F.T.S. 6

You are a human brain, and you've been sending strong signals to your human to warn about the damage caused by bad habits. You've made the human's body feel nauseous, sweaty, achy, and drowsy. You've made its heart race and its head swim. Now, write an e-mail to your human, explaining why you've been putting his or her body through so much trauma. Advise your human to improve habits and reverse the damage. Be sure to stay focused on your topic—and be funny!

Role: a human brain
Audience: the human whose brain you are
Format: an e-mail
Topic: how to reverse the damage it's done by neglecting itself
Strong Verbs: explain, advise

Write your e-mail on a separate sheet of paper. Before you begin to write, jot down some details you might include.

Think About

- Have I zeroed in on one small part of a bigger idea?

- Can I sum up my idea in a simple sentence?

- Have I chosen the information that best captures my idea?

- Have I thought deeply about what the reader will need to know?

Ideas: Focusing the Topic

Jump Start Sheet

Days 1 and 3: My Unit Project To-Do List

- _____

- _____

- _____

- _____

Day 5: My Six-Word Statement on Humor

_____ _____ _____ _____ _____ _____

Focus on Word Study

Root: *dict*

Meaning: _____

Common Words That Contain the Root:

1.

2.

3.

My Wacky Word

_____

_____

_____

_____

Write-On Sheet

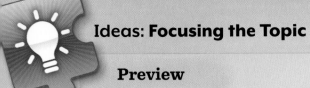

Ideas: **Focusing the Topic**

Seymour Simon, author of *The Brain*

Answer the questions below. Discuss your answers with a partner.

1. Seymour Simon was a teacher before he became a full-time author of science books for young people. How do you think his career as a writer is similar or dissimilar to his work as a teacher?

   _____

   _____

2. Growing up, Seymour Simon lived in the city and spent summers in the country. What do you think each of these environments might have contributed to his writing?

   _____

   _____

3. Some of Seymour Simon's other books include *The Paper Airplane Book, Guts: Our Digestive System, Our Solar System, Animals Nobody Loves*, and *Earthquakes*. Which book would you be most interested in reading?

   _____

   _____

4. If you could write an outstanding science book for middle schoolers, what would your topic be? How about the title?

   _____

   _____

Think Like a Professional Writer

Ideas

1. In the boxes, name six focused ideas that the professional writer your group chose might write about.

Writing Job:

_____

_____

2. Choose your two best writing ideas from the boxes and sum up each one in a simple sentence.

_____

_____

_____

_____

Expository Publishing Checklist

Think you are ready to go public with your expository unit project? Use this form to make sure you've covered all the writing bases.

Writing finished? Check.

Bases covered? Check.

Trait Mate adored? Double check.

I remembered to

☐ include facts that came from reliable sources.

☐ weave in details that show how much I know about my topic.

☐ organize my piece in a way that supports my big idea and makes my message clear.

☐ anticipate and answer readers' questions.

☐ develop the topic logically from beginning to end.

☐ use a voice that expresses my fascination for the topic.

☐ explain any unusual words, phrases, or concepts.

☐ read my piece aloud to check how it will sound to the reader.

☐ proofread my piece carefully and clean up problems with conventions.

The purpose of my piece is to

_____

The part that works the best is

_____

What I hope readers will take away from my piece is

_____

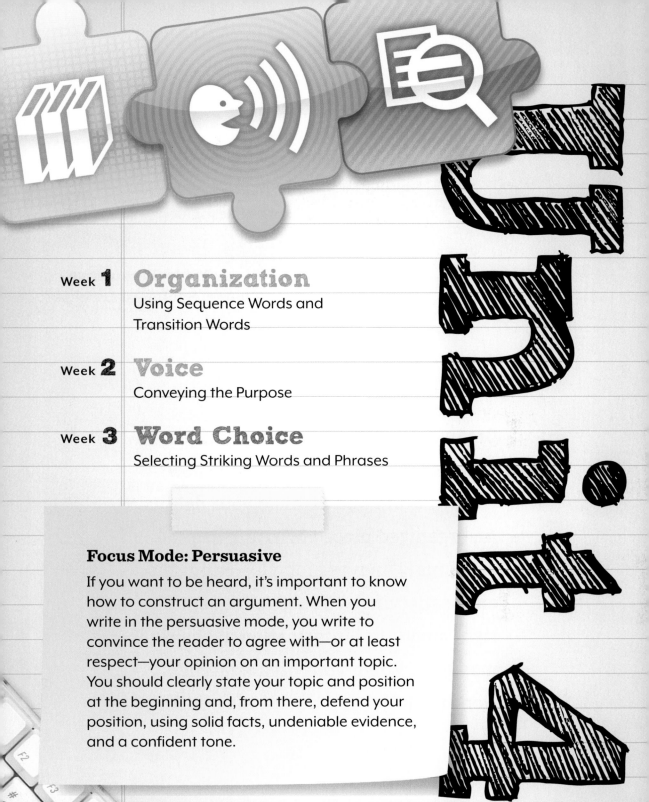

Focus Mode: Persuasive

If you want to be heard, it's important to know
how to construct an argument. When you
write in the persuasive mode, you write to
convince the reader to agree with—or at least
respect—your opinion on an important topic.
You should clearly state your topic and position
at the beginning and, from there, defend your
position, using solid facts, undeniable evidence,
and a confident tone.

- Creating the Lead
- **Using Sequence Words and Transition Words** ⋯⋯⋯⋯⋯⋯⋯⋯
- Structuring the Body
- Ending With a Sense of Resolution

Focus Mode: Persuasive
Theme: Social Awareness

Organization

Organization is about how your idea unfolds from beginning to end—how you structure and arrange your details. An organized piece of writing begins engagingly, moves along logically, and ends satisfyingly. You give readers the right amount of information at the right moments. When your organization is working, following the idea is effortless.

Relay racers never write RUN-on sentences.

Organization

Using Sequence Words and Transition Words

Sequence words (such as *before* and *later*) and transition words (such as *however* and *because*) show how ideas progress, relate, and/or diverge. When you weave sequence and transition words into a piece, your sentences fit together seamlessly. It's easy to see relationships among your ideas.

How is using sequence words and transition words in your writing like handing off the baton in a relay race?

Link It Up!

Using sequence and transition words helps you connect one idea to the next. Read the following sets of words organized by purpose. With a partner, consult a book, magazine, website, or other source to find an example of one word from each set. Write it on the lines below.

To show location: *above, beneath, amid, in back of, beyond, in front of, beside*

_____

_____

To compare or contrast: *similarly, but, however, conversely, even so, otherwise, even though, on the other hand, in the same way*

_____

_____

To show time: *before, earlier, previously, at first, at the same time, meanwhile, soon, then, afterward, after a while, finally*

_____

_____

To add information: *besides, in addition, for example, furthermore, equally important*

_____

_____

To emphasize a point: *again, obviously, undoubtedly, in fact, for this reason, luckily*

_____

To conclude or summarize: *finally, to sum up, to clarify, as a result, in short, in summary, in conclusion*

_____

R.A.F.T.S. 7

As City Parks Commissioner, you were astonished to hear that the mayor's latest budget calls for you to close a community skate park because it is too expensive to maintain. This upsets you because the skate park is one of few places in the city for young people to gather. But you have an idea: If you can get local business owners to donate money to the "Adopt-a-Park" program, you might just be able to keep the park open. It's up to you to convince them. Write a flyer that you know will persuade business owners to support the cause. Pay close attention to using sequence words and transition words.

Role: commissioner of parks and recreation
Audience: local business owners
Format: flyer
Topic: a community skate park that's about to close down
Strong Verbs: convince, persuade

Write your flyer on a separate sheet of paper. Before you begin to write, jot down some details you might include.

Think About

- Have I used sequence words such as *later, then,* and *meanwhile*?

- Did I use a variety of transition words such as *however, because, also,* and *for instance*?

- Have I shown how the ideas connect from sentence to sentence?

- Does my organization make sense from paragraph to paragraph?

Jump Start Sheet

Unit Project Topic: _____

Days 1 and 3: My Unit Project To-Do List

- _____
- _____
- _____
- _____

Day 5: My Six-Word Statement on Awareness

_____ _____ _____ _____ _____ _____

Focus on Grammar and Usage

Search your writing for sentences in which you've used progressive verbs incorrectly. Rewrite two of them correctly here. Or, if you can't find any problems, write two that show you really know what you are doing with progressive verbs.

1. _____

   _____

   _____

2. _____

   _____

   _____

Write-On Sheet

Preview

Patricia T. O'Conner, author of *Woe Is I Jr.*

Answer the questions below on your own or with a partner.

1. Patricia T. O'Conner is a former editor for the *New York Times* Book Review section. How do you think this experience helped her hone her grammar skills?

   _____

   _____

   _____

2. O'Conner has written multiple best-selling books on grammar, and continues to write columns and Op-Ed pieces about grammar for the *New York Times*. Why do you think there is so much public interest in grammar?

   _____

   _____

   _____

3. O'Conner co-writes most of her books with her husband, Stewart Kellerman. Why might it be helpful to collaborate with a partner when writing?

   _____

   _____

   _____

Bonus: Look up Patricia T. O'Conner on the Internet. Write your findings on note cards and share them with a classmate.

Looking for Linking Words

Linkin', linkin',
I've been thinkin'…

Organization

In column 1, list the phrases where you find sequence and transition words in the passage from *Woe Is I Jr.* In column 2, determine the purpose of each word or phrase.

Phrases With Sequence and Transition Words	Purpose
"Before you knew any words at all"	to show time

Now write two sentences from the excerpt that you think demonstrate the most effective use of sequence and transition words.

_____

_____

_____

_____

- Establishing a Tone
- **Conveying the Purpose** ••••••••••••••••••••
- Creating a Connection to the Audience
- Taking Risks to Create Voice

Focus Mode: Persuasive
Theme: Social Awareness

Voice

Voice is the energy and attitude of a piece of writing. In fiction, voice can take on almost any tone, from humorous or hopeful to serious or somber. In nonfiction, it is often compelling, authoritative, and knowledgeable. You arrive at the right voice for a piece by thinking deeply about your purpose and audience for it. You "speak" in a way that connects to your audience.

Conveying the Purpose

My BFF gave me a BWV (bracelet with voice).

The voice you use should match your purpose for writing. For example, if your purpose is to tell a story about a sleepover with a friend, your voice might be upbeat and funny. But you'd use an authoritative voice when writing an expository piece and a convincing one for a persuasive piece. Writers use voice to help readers understand why you have written and why they should care about what you have to say.

How is conveying your purpose to the reader like making the perfect bracelet for a friend?

Voice: **Conveying the Purpose**

What's the Purpose?

Review the three main purposes for writing.

1. **Expository:** to inform or explain

   Possible Voice: knowledgeable, serious

   Typical Formats: Web pages, how-to manuals, magazine articles, research reports

2. **Narrative:** to tell a story or entertain

   Possible Voice: funny, scary, melancholy

   Typical Formats: historical accounts, personal essays, skits, short stories

3. **Persuasive:** to construct an argument

   Possible Voice: confident, convincing

   Typical Formats: advertisements, editorials, and contest entries

For each of the following writing formats/topics, fill in the purpose and the voice you would use to convey that purpose.

essay on the causes and effects of pollution Purpose: _____ Voice: _____	signage on the beach about using trash cans to keep beaches clean Purpose: _____ Voice: _____
explanation of an invention that would make everyday life easier Purpose: _____ Voice: _____	packaging copy for an invention that would make everyday life easier Purpose: _____ Voice: _____
brochure telling how to keep bears away while camping Purpose: _____ Voice: _____	story about a bear encounter while camping Purpose: _____ Voice: _____

R.A.F.T.S. 8

You are the student representative for your school board, and the board members want to change the dress code to require uniforms. You and your classmates have strong feelings against it, mostly because you think their choices are bland, boring, and itchy. You have only one chance to speak up, or you risk getting stuck wearing those uniforms every day, all year. Make your case by outlining the argument you will present at the next board meeting. Be sure to include your reasons for opposing the policy, as well as compromises you would be willing to consider. Be sure your goal, to convince board members to listen to and agree with you, is clearly conveyed.

Role: student representative
Audience: school board members
Format: argument outline
Topic: school uniforms
Strong Verbs: argue, oppose, convince

Write your argument outline on a separate sheet of paper. Before you begin to write, jot down some details you might include.

Think About

- Is the purpose of my writing clear?
- Does my point of view come through?
- Is this the right tone for this kind of writing?
- Have I used strong voice throughout this piece?

Voice: **Conveying the Purpose**

Jump Start Sheet

Days 1 and 3: My Unit Project To-Do List

- _____

- _____

- _____

- _____

Day 5: My Six-Word Statement on Social Awareness

_____ _____ _____ _____ _____ _____

Focus on Word Study

Root: *bio*

Meaning: _____

Common Words That Contain the Root:

1.

2.

3.

My Wacky Word

_____

_____

_____

_____

Write-On Sheet

Voice: **Conveying the Purpose**

Cynthia Lord, author of *Touch Blue*

Answer the questions below on your own or with a partner.

1. Cynthia Lord attributes her success in writing to her love of reading. Why do you think that reading and successful writing go hand in hand?

_____

_____

_____

2. Lord's advice is to write about what you know. For example, she lives along the rocky coast of Maine, the setting for *Touch Blue*. How do you think writing from your own experiences can help you to be a better writer?

_____

_____

_____

3. Lord often tells students to keep daydreaming. How can daydreaming be helpful to writers?

_____

_____

_____

Bonus: Look up on the Internet information about Cynthia Lord. Write your findings on note cards and share them with a classmate.

Vary the Voice

In *Touch Blue*, Tess writes a letter to Aaron's mom using a timid and uncertain voice. Rewrite the letter using a more confident voice.

> And, no, writing in all caps does NOT count as a "more confident voice."

Dear Ms. Spinney,

_____

_____

_____

_____

_____

_____

_____

_____

_____

_____

_____

Sincerely,

Tess Brooks

P.S. _____

P.P.S. _____

P.P.P.S. _____

- Applying Strong Verbs
- **Selecting Striking Words and Phrases** ·························
- Using Specific and Accurate Words
- Choosing Words That Deepen Meaning

Focus Mode: Persuasive
Theme: Social Awareness

Word Choice

Words are the building blocks of writing. Well-chosen words bring your ideas into focus. They create images, spark the imagination, and grab the reader's attention. Word choice is verbal alchemy; it's how writers transform the ordinary into the extraordinary. Choose words that move, enlighten, and inspire.

Selecting Striking Words and Phrases

Can we move off this page, please? I have allergies.

Word Choice

When you use striking words and phrases, readers feel they're inside your idea, rather than on the outside looking in. Striking words and phrases, which include figurative language such as alliteration, simile, and metaphor, add interest and flavor to your writing. Your piece lingers in readers' minds long after they've finished reading it.

How is a piece of writing filled with striking words and phrases similar to a meadow filled with colorful wildflowers?

Brighten Up Your Writing

Review these techniques for selecting striking words and phrases. Then spice up the bland examples by applying the techniques.

Strive for Precise Descriptions

Select words and phrases that perfectly capture what you're describing.

Examples: *bad rainstorm* **vs.** *torrential downpour*
little piece **vs.** *miniscule speck*

My example: good food **vs.** _____

Use Just-Right Compound Adjectives

Hyphenate two or more words to create phrases that say just what you want to say.

Examples: *sure-footed climber, long-winded bore, ice-cold lemonade*

My example: fast car **vs.** _____

Try a Little Alliteration

Tie together words with similar initial sounds so they roll off the tip of your tongue.

Examples: cozy *quarters, steaming stew, busy body*

My example: silly hat **vs.** _____

Emphasize Key Words

<u>Underline</u>, *italicize*, or **boldface** essential words so they stand out from the crowd. (Underlining works best when writing by hand. Use italics and boldface when typing.)

Example: You must always wear a helmet. If you don't, are you *really* a safe cyclist?

My example: I was angry. **vs.** _____

R.A.F.T.S. 9

Lake Lounjahbout is owned and maintained by the Runamuck Development Company, and you pay an annual membership fee to swim and boat there. The members all agree that spending summers by the lake is glorious. But lately, it hasn't been so enjoyable. The water has gotten scummy and leaves a smelly, oily film on your skin. Trash has washed ashore and broken bottles are hidden in the sand of the beaches. You decide to write a petition that members will sign and send to Runamuck. Your petition should express members' love of the lake, detail the pollution problems, and demand that the company clean up. Be sure to select striking words and phrases.

Role: Lake Lounjahbout member
Audience: Runamuck Development Company
Format: petition
Topic: pollution in Lake Lounjahbout
Strong Verbs: detail, express, demand

Create your petition on a separate sheet of paper. Before you begin to write, jot down some details you might include.

Think About

- Did I try to use words that sound *just right*?
- Did I try hyphenating several shorter words to make an interesting-sounding new word?
- Did I try putting words with the same sound together?
- Did I read my piece aloud to find at least one or two moments I love?

Jump Start Sheet

Days 1 and 3: My Unit Project To-Do List

- _____
- _____
- _____
- _____

Day 5: My Six-Word Statement on Social Awareness

_____ _____ _____ _____ _____ _____

Focus on Grammar and Usage

Search your writing for sentences in which you have used subject and object pronouns incorrectly. Rewrite two of them correctly here. Or, if you can't find any problems, write two that show you really know what you are doing with subject and object pronouns.

1. _____
   _____
   _____

2. _____
   _____
   _____

Write-On Sheet

Word Choice: **Selecting Striking Words and Phrases**

A Fund-raiser

Answer the questions below on your own or with a partner.

1. Fund-raisers are responsible for raising money to support important causes such as cancer research, wildlife preservation, and domestic violence prevention. What do you think is the hardest or most interesting part of the job?

   _____

   _____

   _____

2. What skills must a fund-raiser have? Why do you think writing is an important skill for a fund-raiser?

   _____

   _____

   _____

3. Can you name a cause you care about and why you would consider making a donation or devoting time to it?

   _____

   _____

   _____

   _____

   Bonus: Look up on the Internet what a fund-raiser does. Write your findings on note cards and share them with a classmate.

Build a Brochure

My Cause: Summer Camp for Trait Mates

Pick a cause, write a slogan for it, and sketch a logo for it below. Then complete the chart by answering the questions in the left column. Use your answers to write a brochure that will convince people to donate time to the cause.

Cause: _____

Slogan: _____

Who is your target audience?	
What are you trying to accomplish?	
Where is your organization located?	
When are volunteers needed?	
Why is this cause important?	

Create the final version of your brochure on a separate sheet of paper. Don't forget to use striking words and phrases.

Persuasive Publishing Checklist

Think you are ready to go public with your persuasive unit project? Use this form to make sure you've covered all the writing bases.

Very persuasive presentation, my friend!

I remembered to

☐ state my position on the topic clearly and stick with it.

☐ offer good, sound reasoning that the reader can relate to.

☐ back up my argument with solid facts, opinions, and examples that are based on reliable, objective sources.

☐ expose weaknesses in other arguments and positions.

☐ develop my argument using solid reasoning from beginning to end.

☐ explain any unusual words, phrases, or concepts.

☐ read my piece aloud to check how it will sound to the reader.

☐ proofread my piece carefully and clean up problems with conventions.

The purpose of my piece is

_____

The most critical point I make is

_____

_____

What I hope readers will take away from my piece is

_____

_____

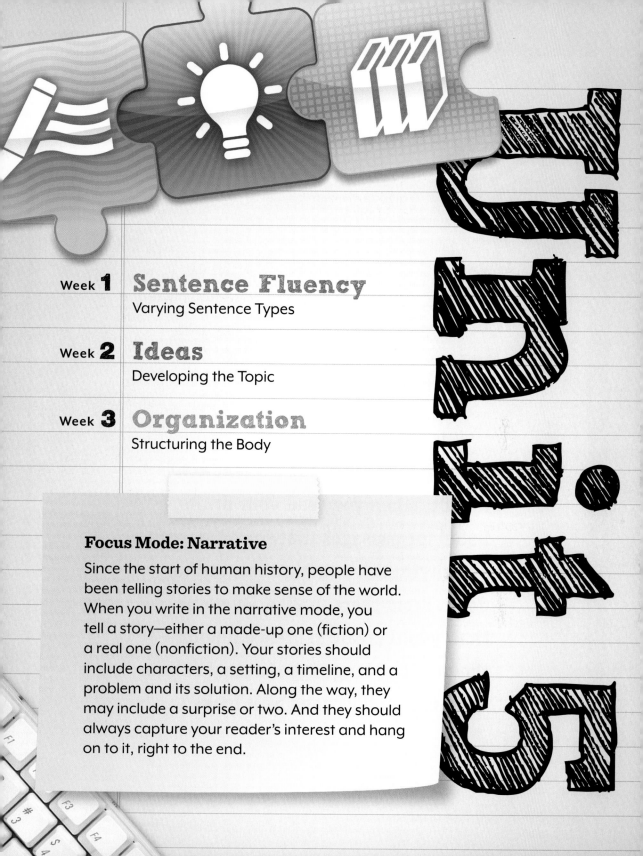

Focus Mode: Narrative

Since the start of human history, people have been telling stories to make sense of the world. When you write in the narrative mode, you tell a story—either a made-up one (fiction) or a real one (nonfiction). Your stories should include characters, a setting, a timeline, and a problem and its solution. Along the way, they may include a surprise or two. And they should always capture your reader's interest and hang on to it, right to the end.

- Crafting Well-Built Sentences
- **Varying Sentence Types** . . . .
- Capturing Smooth and Rhythmic Flow
- Breaking the "Rules" to Create Fluency

Focus Mode: Narrative
Theme: Patience

Sentence Fluency

Writing may seem like a silent act, but it isn't. When you read your drafts, listen for passages that sound smooth and rhythmic . . . and passages that don't. From there, revise. By doing that, you'll create sentence fluency— the music of language that makes your writing sound as good as it looks.

Varying Sentence Types

What if every piece of writing you pick up contained sentences following the same pattern: adjective, noun, verb, adverb? Bor-*ing*! A monotonous rhythm distracts you from the content and lulls you to sleep. Now, imagine a piece that flows smoothly through simple, compound, and complex sentences and uses a variety of statements, questions, and exclamations. Using careful selection of different forms of sentences to enhance meaning and create flow can make or break how your writing sounds to the reader.

How is varying sentence types in writing like playing with a yo-yo?

Mix It Up

Varying the types of sentences you use keeps your writing flowing and easy on the ear. Here are four different types that you can use, along with an explanation of the clauses and phrases that are used to build sentences.

Types of Sentences

1. **Simple**: a sentence made up of one independent clause

   Example: The girl rode the bus. She waited at the corner.

2. **Compound**: a sentence made up of two or more independent clauses joined by a conjunction such as *and, but,* or *or*

   Example: The girl waited at the corner, but the bus was late.

3. **Complex**: a sentence made up of an independent clause and at least one dependent clause

   Example: While the girl waited for the bus, she sent a text to a friend.

4. **Compound-Complex**: a sentence made up of two or more independent clauses and at least one dependent clause

   Example: When the girl's friend replied, he invited her to a party, and she happily accepted the invitation.

Clauses and Phrases

A **clause** is a sentence part that contains a subject and a verb.

1. An **independent clause** can stand alone as a correct sentence.

   Example: She rode the bus.

2. A **dependent clause** cannot stand alone.

   Example: After she got off the bus . . .

A **phrase** is a sentence part that does not contain a subject and verb. Like a dependent clause, it cannot stand alone.

   Example: On Monday

R.A.F.T.S. 10

You have just completed three months as a PaxMundus volunteer in southern Egypt. Now you're on your way to see the Egyptian Nile and Pyramids at Giza. Your budget is small, so you've opted to use ground transportation—but didn't realize that by "seven," the guide meant *days*, not hours; and that by "caravan" didn't mean in a Dodge, it meant on camelback. To make the most of it, you decide to keep a journal, which you will later post to your blog for friends and family. Write one entry, detailing a day from your journey. Be sure to use a variety of sentence types to describe your experience.

Role: traveler
Audience: yourself, friends, and family
Format: blog entry
Topic: unexpected seven-day camel caravan ride
Strong Verbs: detail, describe

Write your blog entry on a separate sheet of paper. Before you begin to write, jot down some details you might include.

Think About

- Do I include different kinds of sentences?
- Are some of my sentences complex?
- Are some of my sentences simple?
- Did I intermingle sentence types, one to the next?

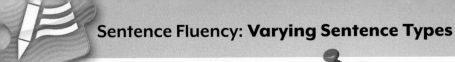

Jump Start Sheet

Unit Project Topic: _____

Days 1 and 3: My Unit Project To-Do List

- _____

- _____

- _____

- _____

Day 5: My Six-Word Statement on Patience

_____ _____ _____ _____ _____ _____

Focus on Word Study

Root: *ject*
Meaning: _____
Common Words That Contain the Root:

1.

2.

3.

My Wacky Word

_____

_____

_____

_____

Write-On Sheet

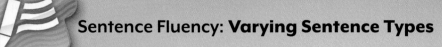

Preview

Lisa Yee, author of
Stanford Wong Flunks Big-Time

Answer the questions below on your own or with a partner.

1. Lisa Yee had many different jobs before becoming an author of books for young people, including advertising copywriter, journalist, and television writer. Which of these three jobs do you think best prepared her for writing humorous young adult books?

   _____

   _____

2. Some writing ideas just "hit" Lisa Yee, while others had to "brew" in her brain for a while. Sometimes they come from observing the world and taking notes. How do you come up with your ideas?

   _____

   _____

3. Lisa Yee says that in order to be a good writer, you must also be a good reader. How do you think reading helps your writing?

   _____

   _____

4. Lisa Yee often talks to students about being a successful writer. If she came to your school, what would you ask her?

   _____

   _____

Sentence Remix

After your partner "remixes" your writing with new types of sentences, complete the chart below. Find an example of each sentence type. Then read them aloud to your partner.

1. Write one or more **simple sentences**.

_____

_____

_____

_____

2. Write one or more **compound sentences**. Underline each independent clause. Circle each conjunction.

_____

_____

_____

_____

3. Write one or more **complex sentences**. Draw one line under each independent clause. Draw two lines under each dependent clause.

_____

_____

_____

4. Write one or more **compound-complex sentences**. Draw one line under each independent clause. Draw two lines under each dependent clause. Circle each conjunction.

_____

_____

_____

- Finding a Topic
- Focusing the Topic
- **Developing the Topic** ....
- Using Details

Focus Mode: Narrative
Theme: Patience

Ideas

Ideas are your central message—the main thoughts you want to share. To make your ideas strong, choose a topic you care about and focus on one interesting aspect of it. From there, weave in original and unexpected details to open your readers' eyes and show them something they might otherwise overlook.

Developing the Topic

This guy's sure getting "a head" in the sculpting business.

When you develop your topic, you expand your main idea in a logical direction. You give your story an original, unpredictable plot with a problem to be resolved. In nonfiction, you present accurate facts, anecdotes, and examples to explain the main idea. When the topic is well developed, your readers become engaged in the content: their questions are answered and their interest is piqued.

How is developing the topic like sculpting a work of art?

The Plot Thickens

A good plot starts with a great idea. Then the writer develops that idea with characters, a setting (place and time), and a conflict and resolution. Here's how to get things rolling.

1. **Introduce the plot and lay the groundwork for the conflict.**

   Describe the character's problem. Start with an event that makes the problem clear and causes the character to take action.

   Example: *Shyla had always been terrified of bugs, but it was no big deal until her science teacher, Ms. Crawly, said two words: "insect investigation."*

2. **Develop the plot and characters; reveal the conflict.**

   Use events to tell how the problem develops and what the character does to solve the problem. He or she might meet friends and enemies, face challenges, or take risks.

   Example: *Shyla couldn't imagine actually touching bugs, so she talked her little brother Max into capturing them for her. They began to search the tall, deep grass behind their house.*

3. **Describe the climax or turning point.**

   Focus on the big event, the most exciting—and important—part of your story. Put your character in a life-changing situation.

   Example: *Shyla felt a tickle on her calf and shrieked at Max. "Stop that!" But when she heard him several feet away, she realized he wasn't the culprit. She looked down in horror at the huge grasshopper on her leg.*

4. **Resolve the conflict and wrap it up.**

   Show how the problem is resolved and tie up loose ends. Share conclusions or lessons learned by the character.

   Example: *Shyla took a deep breath and swiped it off her leg. It landed a few feet away. Watching it, she realized she'd made it through the encounter without a scratch. Maybe grasshoppers weren't so bad, after all.*

R.A.F.T.S. 11

You are a senior citizen who witnessed the arrest of the infamous American frontier outlaw, Six-Eyed Jack Amity, in 1913. There are multiple legends about just how Jack was betrayed by his brother-in-law, Billy Muteny, and captured outside the Hootnanny Hotel in Treetail, Kansas, that night, but no one tells it quite the way you remember it. You've decided to record the story. Remember to use an interesting, believable story line and put your reader right in the action.

Role: senior citizen, born before 1913
Audience: American public
Format: memoir
Topic: the arrest of Six-Eyed Jack Amity
Strong Verbs: tell, record

Write your memoir on a separate sheet of paper. Before you begin to write, jot down some details you might include.

Think About

- Am I sure my information is right?

- Are my details chock-full of interesting information?

- Have I used details that show new thinking about this idea?

- Will my reader believe what I say about this topic?

Ideas: **Developing the Topic**

Jump Start Sheet

Unit Project Topic: _____

Days 1 and 3: My Unit Project To-Do List

- _____

- _____

- _____

- _____

Day 5: My Six-Word Statement on Patience

_____ _____ _____ _____ _____ _____

Focus on Grammar and Usage

Review your writing, find sentences in which you've used homophones incorrectly, and revise two of those sentences here.

1. _____

   _____

   _____

   _____

2. _____

   _____

   _____

   _____

Write-On Sheet

Ideas: **Developing the Topic**

Marina Budhos, author of
Ask Me No Questions

Answer the questions below on your own or with a partner.

1. Marina Budhos has said that her worst flaw is her impatience and her best quality is her patience. How can a writer be both patient and impatient at the same time?

   _____

   _____

   _____

2. One talent Marina Budhos would like to have is the ability to take great photographs. How could that complement her work as a writer?

   _____

   _____

3. When asked if she had any advice for aspiring authors, Marina Budhos once said, "Keep at it." What do you think she meant by that?

   _____

   _____

4. Another of Marina Budhos's books is titled *Remix: Conversations With Immigrant Teenagers*. Why do you think Budhos chose to write from the perspective of teens from different countries?

   _____

   _____

What's Your Story?

A story map?
How about story GPS?
This is the 21st century!

Find a partner and use the story map to plan a story about a time you got exactly what you wished for, but in an unexpected way.

Characters	Setting

Introduce the plot and type of conflict: Person vs. Person / Person vs. Him- or Herself / Person vs. Nature

Develop the characters and plot with revealing events.

Create the climax, or turning point.

Resolve the conflict and tie up loose ends.

- Creating the Lead
- Using Sequence Words and Transition Words
- **Structuring the Body** ••••••••••••••••••••••••••••••
- Ending With a Sense of Resolution

Focus Mode: Narrative
Theme: Patience

Organization

Organization is about how your idea unfolds from beginning to end—how you structure and arrange your details. An organized piece of writing begins engagingly, moves along logically, and ends satisfyingly. You give readers the right amount of information at the right moments. When your organization is working, following the idea is effortless.

Structuring the Body

Bee prepared for some sweet organization!

When you structure the body of a piece of writing, you start with a foundation—the main idea. From there, you build the piece by fitting details together carefully and logically. You slow down your pace when you want readers to ponder a point and speed up when you want to move them along. And you wrap up in just the right place—so you don't ramble on and on like a day that never seems to end!

How is structuring the body of a piece of writing like building a beehive?

Time With a Twist

Here are a few ideas for structuring the body of a piece of narrative writing. Although most narratives use a chronological, or linear, time structure, sometimes writers dip in and out of linear sequence to make the story more complex and interesting. For example:

1. **Flashback**

   The logical progression of events is altered by going back in time instead of forward.

   Example: Shiloh's head swam with nostalgia. Suddenly, she was back in her old bedroom, her plastic tea set on the bedside table, and Reginald the bear seated snugly in her lap.

2. **Fast-forward**

   The natural progression of events is interrupted by a leap ahead in time.

   Example: Five years later, Jamal realized that what he had seen that night was critical to solving the case, and he took his journal, notes, and photographs to the Chief of Detectives.

3. **Repeating Motif**

   There is a recurring element in the story that affects the time sequence.

   Example: Again the same horrible stomachache. Dustin's mind raced. What had he eaten tonight? What had he eaten at the class party? What was going on that was making him so sick? How could he sort it all out?

4. **Full Circle**

   The story begins and ends in the same time frame, shifting time frames in between.

   Example: Seetha began to smile as she opened up the first pages of the just-now-found-but-once-lost-forever book. She began to read the familiar lines, "Once upon a time...."

R.A.F.T.S. 12

You are the Big Bad Wolf, from the fairy tale "Little Red Riding Hood." Rather than being killed at the end of the tale, as some stories report, you actually escaped into the woods where you have lived ever since, waiting patiently for the right time to recount your side of the story. Now *Enchanted Today* magazine has contacted you to do an interview for a feature story. Write an oral interview in which you give the tabloid interviewer your side of the tale. Remember to organize the body of your piece in a clear and interesting way.

Role: Big Bad Wolf
Audience: *Enchanted Today* readers
Format: oral interview
Topic: "Little Red Riding Hood"—*your* version
Strong Verbs: report, recount

Write your interview on a separate sheet of paper. Before you begin to write, jot down some ideas you might include.

Think About

- Have I shown the reader where to slow down and where to speed up?
- Do all the details fit where they are placed?
- Will the reader find it easy to follow my ideas?
- Does the organization help the main idea stand out?

Jump Start Sheet

Unit Project Topic: _____

Days 1 and 3: My Unit Project To-Do List

- _____
- _____
- _____
- _____

Day 5: My Six-Word Statement on Patience

_____ _____ _____ _____ _____ _____

Focus on Word Study

Root: *graph*
Meaning: _____

Common Words That Contain the Root:

1.

2.

3.

My Wacky Word

_____

_____

_____

_____

Write-On Sheet

Preview

A Cartoonist

Answer the questions below on your own or with a partner.

1. A cartoonist communicates in words and pictures. Which do you think would be more challenging—words or pictures?

_____

_____

_____

_____

2. A good cartoon makes us laugh. What makes cartoons funny?

_____

_____

_____

_____

3. Describe a cartoon or comic that you remember. Why does it stick in your mind?

_____

_____

_____

_____

Bonus: Look up on the Internet what a cartoonist does. Write your findings on note cards and share them with a classmate.

Comic Creator

What do you call someone who's sick of us Trait Mates? Puzz-ill!

Answer the questions below to help you create an eight-panel sequel to the *Sherman's Lagoon* comic strip.

1. What will your comic strip be about? What joke, play on words, or other idea will be the focus of your comic strip?

_____

2. **Panel 1:** How will your comic strip begin? Write a brief description of what will occur in the first panel. Engage the reader from the get-go!

_____

_____

3. **Panels 2–7:** Get organized! Figure out the chronological structure of your cartoon. Sort out how it develops in the middle. Decide whether you want to try any time twists.

   Panel 2: _____

   Panel 3: _____

   Panel 4: _____

   Panel 5: _____

   Panel 6: _____

   Panel 7: _____

4. **Panel 8:** How will your comic strip end? Write a brief description of what will occur in the last panel. Create an ending that helps readers get the joke and makes them smile.

_____

_____

_____

Narrative Publishing Checklist

Think you are ready to go public with your narrative unit project? Use this form to make sure you've covered all the writing bases.

I remembered to...

- ☐ present a clear, well-developed story line.
- ☐ include fascinating characters that grow and change over time.
- ☐ convey time and setting that make sense for the story.
- ☐ entertain, surprise, and challenge the reader.
- ☐ develop the story chronologically or take a risk to try a structure that also helps the reader follow the story easily.
- ☐ use an active voice to engage the reader.
- ☐ choose words that fit the characters, time, and place.
- ☐ read my piece aloud to check for places where I should speed up or slow down.
- ☐ proofread my piece carefully and clean up problems with conventions.

The purpose of my piece is

_____

My favorite part is

_____

What I hope readers will find most memorable about my piece is

_____

> Great story line. Flawless conventions. And it's easy to dance to. I give it a 10!

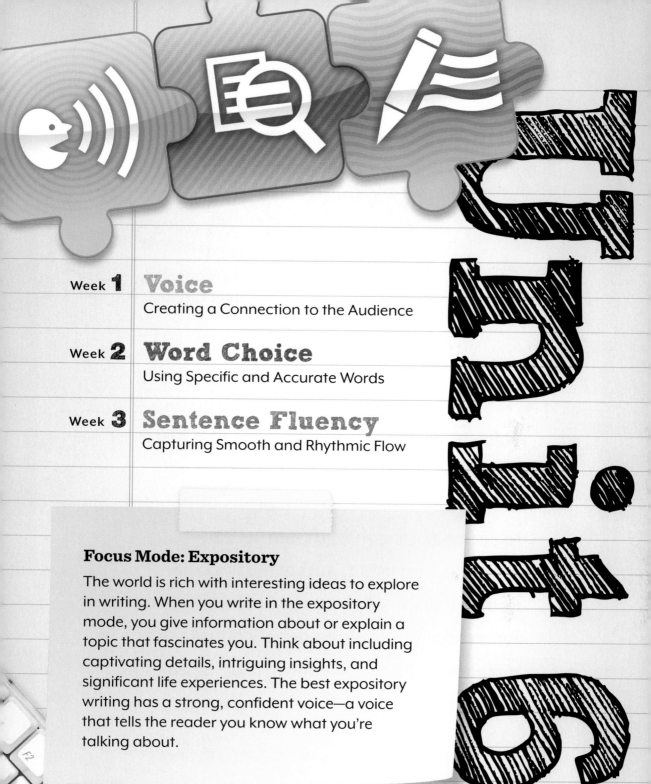

Focus Mode: Expository

The world is rich with interesting ideas to explore in writing. When you write in the expository mode, you give information about or explain a topic that fascinates you. Think about including captivating details, intriguing insights, and significant life experiences. The best expository writing has a strong, confident voice—a voice that tells the reader you know what you're talking about.

- Establishing a Tone
- Conveying the Purpose
- **Creating a Connection to the Audience** ....
- Taking Risks to Create Voice

Focus Mode: Expository
Theme: Curiosity

Voice

Voice is the energy and attitude of a piece of writing. In fiction, voice can take on almost any tone, from humorous or hopeful to serious or somber. In nonfiction, it is often compelling, authoritative, and knowledgeable. You arrive at the right voice for a piece by thinking deeply about your purpose and audience for it. You "speak" in a way that connects to your audience.

Creating a Connection to the Audience

Who's better at making connections than us puzzle pieces?

Voice

When you're speaking to your friends, you probably use different language and a different tone than when you're speaking to your English teacher. The same principle applies to writing. By saying just the right things in just the right way, you connect to readers. You make them want to listen and take your message seriously.

How is creating a connection to the audience in writing like performing on a stage?

Making the Connection

Here are two student essays of the same length on the same topic. One of them creates a strong connection to the audience. The other does not. Use **The Who**, **The How**, and **The Why** techniques you learned to think about why one works better than the other.

1. **Charles's Room**

   Charles's room is on the second story of his house. It is 120 square feet with one window overlooking the yard. On the floor is a beige carpet. On the walls are posters of his favorite athletes. Charles's baseball glove sits atop a high bookshelf in the corner. On top of a desk are a laptop computer, a calendar, and a small collection of action figures. The desk is against the wall beneath the window, with a bed on the other side of the room. Charles comes here to sleep, do homework, find privacy, and daydream. This room and its things are important to Charles. He has lived here for 12 years.

   _____

2. **A Room of His Own**

   Charles comes in the back door, feeds the dog, and heads to his room. It's not very big, and until his brother David went to college last year he had to share it. But now it's his haven, a place that he can go at the end of the day and unwind. He falls onto the bed, grabs his headphones and listens to music. As he's lying there he studies the posters of basketball and football heroes, action figures he can't seem to give up even though it's been years since he's played with them, and his collection of rocks from camping trips and vacations. His room is filled with memories that give him a sense of belonging. Surrounded by the things he loves, Charles's eyes begin to close. "I'll just take a little nap," he thinks, "before I start my homework."

   _____

   • Which paper makes a stronger connection to the reader? _____
   • Which techniques do you think the writer of the stronger paper used?

   _____

   • What technique would help improve the weaker paper?

   _____

R.A.F.T.S. 13

You are a meteorologist, a scientist who studies weather. A major storm—showering record-breaking hailstones the size of grapefruits—has just hit a town a few miles away. You have approximately 20 minutes before it hits your city. Write a TV emergency weather alert for viewers in your area, warning them of the oncoming storm, telling them of its dangers, and explaining what they can do to protect their property and stay safe. Be sure to create a connection that will capture your audience's attention.

Role: meteorologist
Audience: TV viewers
Format: emergency weather alert
Topic: approaching hailstorm
Strong Verbs: alert, warn, explain

Write your alert on a separate sheet of paper. Before you begin to write, jot down some details you might include.

Think About

- Have I thought about the reader?
- Is this the right voice for the audience?
- Have I shown what matters most to me in this piece?
- Will the reader know how I think and feel about the topic?

Jump Start Sheet

Unit Project Topic: _____

Days 1 and 3: My Unit Project To-Do List

- _____
- _____
- _____
- _____

Day 5: My Six-Word Statement on Curiosity

_____ _____ _____ _____ _____ _____

Focus on Grammar and Usage

Search your writing for sentences in which you used regular or irregular verb forms incorrectly. Then revise two of those sentences here.

1. _____

_____

_____

2. _____

_____

_____

Write-On Sheet

Voice: **Creating a Connection to the Audience**

Kris Hirschmann, author of
Wild Weather

Answer the questions below, on your own or with a partner.

1. Kris Hirschmann's two children are her first audience. Why do you think their feedback on her writing, including her voice, is valuable to her?

   _____

   _____

   _____

2. Hirschmann writes mostly for tweens and young teens. Considering the title of the mentor text, what do you think she enjoys about writing for that audience?

   _____

   _____

   _____

3. Hirschmann often visits schools to talk to students about writing and publishing. What is something about nonfiction writing you'd like to hear her talk about if she visited your school?

   _____

   _____

   _____

   Bonus: Look up information about Kris Hirschmann on the Internet. Write your findings on note cards and share them with a classmate.

How to . . .

With a partner, write a paragraph describing how to do something you do every day. Be sure to use voice to create a connection to your audience.

Make 'em laugh, make 'em cry, make 'em beg for more.

Topic: _____

Audience: _____

Our Paragraph:

_____

_____

_____

_____

_____

_____

_____

_____

_____

_____

_____

Strategies we used to connect to the audience:

_____

_____

_____

_____

- Applying Strong Verbs
- Selecting Striking Words and Phrases
- **Using Specific and Accurate Words** ··············
- Choosing Words That Deepen Meaning

Focus Mode: Expository
Theme: Curiosity

Word Choice

Words are the building blocks of writing.
Well-chosen words bring your ideas
into focus. They create images, spark
the imagination, and grab the reader's
attention. Word choice is verbal alchemy;
it's how writers transform the ordinary
into the extraordinary. Choose words
that move, enlighten, and inspire.

Using Specific and Accurate Words

Specific and accurate words give readers the information they need to understand your writing. For example, saying "The fish has many teeth" doesn't grab the reader like this does: "The great white shark has hundreds of razor-sharp teeth arranged in rows." Using words like these puts bite into your piece!

How is using specific and accurate words like skywriting?

Word Choice: **Using Specific and Accurate Words**

How to Become a Wordsmith

Choosing the right words is no easy task. But here are some ideas you can try to find just the right word to express yourself in just the right way.

1. Seek synonyms.

Use a dictionary or thesaurus to find different ways to express an important idea.

Example: You want to describe the spicy taste of an enchilada, so you look up *spicy* and find the synonyms *pungent, hot*, and *savory*. Now you have a more complete menu of words to choose from.

2. Pounce on pitiful words.

Replace vague words such as *good, bad, nice, cool,* or *very* with words that express ideas more precisely.

Example: Instead of writing, "The movie was cool," you might write, "The movie had me on the edge of my seat the whole time!"

3. Modify for meaning.

A well-placed modifier (an adjective or adverb) helps readers picture your ideas. Modifiers can help you express something more accurately than you may be able to do with nouns or verbs alone.

Example: "We sat and watched the sunset" has no modifiers. "We sat motionless and watched the blazing orange sunset" uses modifiers to paint a more precise and vivid picture.

4. Consider connotations.

Words that mean almost the same thing may have different connotations, or shades of meaning. When choosing a word for a piece of writing, think deeply about its definition. What does it *really* mean?

Example: You could say, "The meal was tasty." Or you could say, "The meal was savory." Which was it: "tasty" or "savory"? There is a difference.

R.A.F.T.S. 14

You own the Tangerine Umbrella newsstand in the sprawling city of Hapihagen. You just noticed a group of tourists peering at the street signs. Now they're walking toward you. Looks like they're lost! Take a few moments to list the directions the confused vacationers will need to reach their destination: the Megalith Stadium, on the other side of the city. You might also map out the route by quickly sketching the major streets as well as any different forms of transportation they could take to get there easily. Remember to use specific and accurate words to ensure that the tourists don't get lost again.

Role: Tangerine Umbrella newsstand owner
Audience: group of lost tourists
Format: directions
Topic: how to get from the Tangerine Umbrella to Megalith Stadium
Strong Verbs: list, map out, sketch

Write your directions on a separate sheet of paper. Before you begin to write, jot down some details you might include.

Think About

- Have I used nouns and modifiers that help the reader see a picture?
- Do I avoid using words that might confuse a reader?
- Did I try a new word and, if so, check to make sure I used it correctly?
- Are these the best words that can be used?

Word Choice: **Using Specific and Accurate Words**

Jump Start **Sheet**

Days 1 and 3: My Unit Project To-Do List

- _____
- _____
- _____
- _____

Day 5: My Six-Word Statement on Curiosity

_____   _____   _____   _____   _____   _____

Focus on Word Study

Root: *port*
Meaning: _____
Common Words That Contain the Root:

1.

2.

3.

My Wacky Word

_____

_____

_____

_____

Write-On Sheet

Word Choice: **Using Specific and Accurate Words**

A Curator

Answer the questions below, on your own or with a partner.

1. What do you know about the job of a curator? Why do you think museums rely on curators?

   _____

   _____

   _____

   _____

2. To write a brochure for a museum, what kind of information would a curator want to include?

   _____

   _____

   _____

   _____

3. How might a curator use a brochure to draw visitors in? How might he or she mix information with entertainment?

   _____

   _____

   _____

   _____

Bonus: Look up on the Internet what a curator does. Write your findings on note cards and share them with a classmate.

Recipe for a School Like No Other

Answer the questions below. Then, on a separate sheet of paper, use your answers to write a recipe for a school like no other.

School name: _____

1. What are three things that would make this school a perfect place?

   _____

   _____

   _____

2. What are two unusual things that happen at this school that set it apart from other schools?

   _____

   _____

3. What are some personality traits of the teachers and administrators at this school?

   _____

   _____

4. What are some personality traits of the students at this school?

   _____

   _____

5. What headline would you write for a newspaper article about this school?

   _____

   _____

   _____

- Crafting Well-Built Sentences
- Varying Sentence Types
- **Capturing Smooth and Rhythmic Flow** ....
- Breaking the "Rules" to Create Fluency

Focus Mode: Expository
Theme: Curiosity

Sentence Fluency

Writing may seem like a silent act, but it isn't. When you read your drafts, listen for passages that sound smooth and rhythmic . . . and passages that don't. From there, revise. By doing that, you'll create sentence fluency— the music of language that makes your writing sound as good as it looks.

Capturing Smooth and Rhythmic Flow

You want smooth and rhythmic? Point me to the roller rink.

Good writers revise sentences until they get them right. Their goal? To create a piece that is so smooth and rhythmic it sounds musical. Good writers add, move, and remove words, and then listen for how sentences sound individually and together. Create smooth-sounding sentences. Catch the rhythm of your writing.

How is playing table tennis like capturing smooth and rhythmic flow in writing?

Elegant Prose

Writers use many skills to create smooth and flowing text. Here are some techniques to try as you write elegant sentences that are easy to listen to.

1. Mix 'em Up	Use sentences of different lengths. Example: *It felt like the weekend would never get here. Before I could unwind and have some downtime I still had three tests, basketball practice, and a dentist appointment.*
2. Get to the Point	Don't use unnecessary words. Example: (rambling) *Students are reminded that they are required to arrive at class at the correct hour and to bring all the recommended books, assignments, and materials with them so they are ready to get started immediately.* (clear) *Come to class prepared and on time.*
3. Be Parallel	Use the same construction for similar sentence elements. Example: (tangents) *My backpack was crammed with books, plus in the bottom it had some shoes that I use for gym class, inside were some leftover sandwiches, and I also use my backpack to keep my laptop and cell phone.* (parallel) *My backpack was crammed—it had books, gym shoes, leftover sandwiches, my laptop, and my cell phone.*
4. Use Variety	Vary sentence types to vary the sound of writing. Example: (same type) *I ate too much. I went to bed. I had bad dreams. I woke up. It was only a dream.* (varied) *Sometimes, when I have too much to eat before bedtime, I have bad dreams. I wake up and ask myself, "Was that a dream or was it real?" It's always a relief to realize it was nothing more than a pizza-binge nightmare.*

R.A.F.T.S. 15

You are a carnivorous wild animal in a community of herbivores and have been accused of a vicious crime: snacking on your neighbors! You have been brought before the wild animal tribunal to defend yourself. If found guilty, you will be sent to the zoo. Prepare the segment of your defense that describes your species, habitat, daily (or nightly) schedule, what you are genetically programmed to eat, and why you eat it. Present the facts in a fluid, interesting manner that will (you hope) relate enough about your species to inspire understanding of your plight.

Role: a carnivorous wild animal
Audience: the wild animal tribunal
Format: a defense
Topic: facts about your species' way of life
Strong Verbs: describe, present, relate

Write your defense on a separate sheet of paper. Before you begin to write, jot down some details you might include.

Think About

- Is it easy to read the entire piece aloud?
- Do my sentences flow, one to the next?
- Do individual passages sound smooth when I read them aloud?
- Did I place different sentence types thoughtfully in order to enhance the main idea?

Jump Start Sheet

Days 1 and 3: My Unit Project To-Do List

- _____
- _____
- _____
- _____

Day 5: My Six-Word Statement on Curiosity

_____ _____ _____ _____ _____ _____

Focus on Grammar and Usage

Search your writing for sentences with direct objects. Write two of the sentences here. Circle the direct objects.

1. _____

_____

_____

_____

2. _____

_____

_____

_____

Write-On Sheet

Preview

Pam Muñoz Ryan, author of
Esperanza Rising

Answer the questions below, on your own or with a partner.

1. Ryan says that her main goal as a writer is getting the reader to "turn the page." Name some ways writers entice you to turn the page.

   _____

   _____

   _____

2. As a girl, Ryan spent a lot of time at her grandmother's house, listening to stories. How might hearing stories help a future writer?

   _____

   _____

   _____

3. Ryan is a writer who uses her work to explore what she is curious about. Name a curiosity you've developed recently—one that never would have occurred to you when you were younger. Why is it important to you?

   _____

   _____

   _____

Bonus: Find one or two more facts about Pam Muñoz Ryan on the Internet. Share them with a classmate.

Fluency Fumble

Mess with great literature? Why not? Choose a smoothly flowing paragraph from Pam Muñoz Ryan's *Esperanza Rising* and transform it into a rough, clunky, poorly flowing paragraph. Techniques you might use:

- Begin sentences the same way.
- Structure sentences the same way (noun-verb-direct object, for example).
- Make all sentences the same length.

Um ... If Pam Muñoz Ryan walks in, turn the page—quickly!

Expository Publishing Checklist

Think you are ready to go public with your expository unit project? Use this form to make sure you've covered all the writing bases.

Nice work! Now if you'll excuse me, I'm off to the Conventions convention.

I remembered to

☐ include facts and information that came from reliable sources.

☐ weave in details that show how much I know about my topic.

☐ develop the topic logically from beginning to end.

☐ use a voice that expresses my fascination for the topic.

☐ explain any unusual words, phrases, or concepts.

☐ read my piece aloud to check how it will sound to the readers.

☐ proofread my piece carefully and clean up problems with conventions.

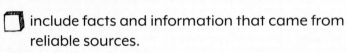

The purpose of my piece is

_____

_____

The part that works the best is

_____

_____

What I hope readers will take away from my piece is

_____

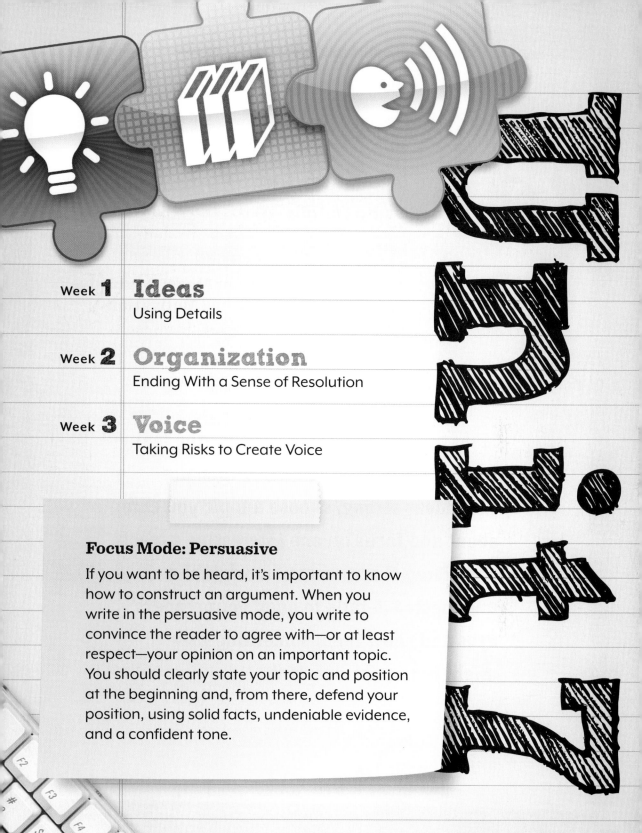

Focus Mode: Persuasive

If you want to be heard, it's important to know how to construct an argument. When you write in the persuasive mode, you write to convince the reader to agree with—or at least respect—your opinion on an important topic. You should clearly state your topic and position at the beginning and, from there, defend your position, using solid facts, undeniable evidence, and a confident tone.

- Finding a Topic
- Focusing the Topic
- Developing the Topic
- **Using Details** ....

Focus Mode: Persuasive
Theme: Motivation

Ideas

Ideas are your central message—the main thoughts you want to share. To make your ideas strong, choose a topic you care about and focus on one interesting aspect of it. From there, weave in original and unexpected details to open your readers' eyes and show them something they might otherwise overlook.

Using Details

Vivid, accurate details take your work from *ho-hum* to *how about that*! You draw the reader in by describing how things look, taste, feel, sound, and smell. Stretching to find, for example, a little-known fact or to create a complex character puts readers in the moment with you—and once they get a taste of what you have to say, they'll hang onto your every word.

Those mosaics think they're so superior to us jigsaw puzzles. Drives me crazy!

Ideas

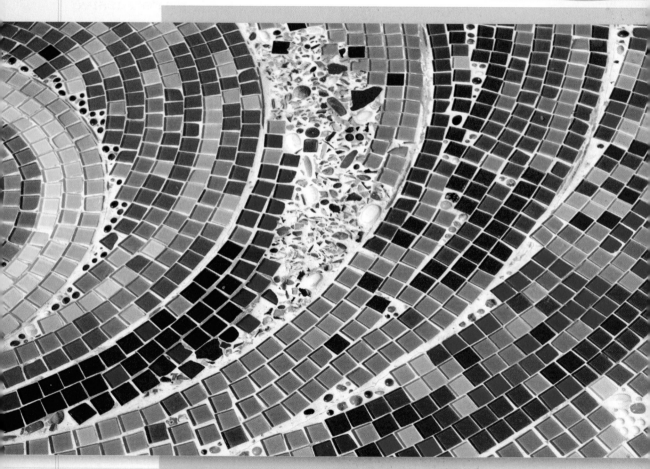

How is using details in writing like creating a mosaic design?

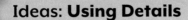

Choosing and Using High-Quality Details

How can you make sure that you're including the best details in your writing? Details that are interesting, focused, and believable? Here are some tips.

1. **Draw upon your own knowledge.** Use experiences and anecdotes from your life.

   Example: Have you ever heard a jackhammer? Well, I have: I woke up one morning with an earsplitting sound rattling the windows in my bedroom and making my jaw throb. When I looked out, I saw they were repairing the pothole in our street.

2. **Ask yourself questions about your topic.** Gather information and evidence from reliable sources to answer those questions.

   Example: Are there places to stay at the bottom of the Grand Canyon? The recently renovated Phantom Ranch and Spa at the very bedrock of the Grand Canyon offers luxurious and relaxing cabins for adventurous hikers and mule riders who brave the canyon trails.

3. **Zero in on important points.** Don't clutter your writing with unimportant details.

   Example: Freezing rain often turns city streets into stretches of treacherous, ice-glazed asphalt. ~~that are far more dangerous than the ice skating rink that tourists love to visit at New York City's Rockefeller Center.~~

4. **Scratch below the surface.** Stretch for details that go beyond the commonplace or obvious.

   Example: Spring is leafy and lush, with the rich smells of earthworm-tilled flower beds, blossoming plum trees, and freshly mowed fescue. Sadly, though, what makes spring wonderful also makes our eyes water and noses run: pollen.

R.A.F.T.S. 16

You've recently started a Web-based business—Hats of Hazzard. From the fabulously chic to the wild and crazy, your business sells the most interesting headgear on the worldwide market. As an online retailer, capturing the interest of Internet shoppers is one of your biggest challenges, so you've decided to take out some ad space on a few of your favorite websites. Create a sidebar ad that will appeal to prospective customers. Use high-quality details to motivate them to click the link to *your* website.

Role: online business owner
Audience: prospective customers
Format: website sidebar ad
Topic: Hats of Hazzard website
Strong Verbs: appeal, motivate, persuade

Write your ad on a separate sheet of paper. Before you begin to write, jot down some details you might include.

Think About

- Did I create a picture in the reader's mind?
- Did I use details that draw upon the five senses (sight, touch, taste, smell, hearing)?
- Do my details stay on the main topic?
- Did I stretch for details beyond the obvious?

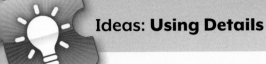

Jump Start Sheet

Unit Project Topic: _____

Days 1 and 3: My Unit Project To-Do List

- _____
- _____
- _____
- _____

Day 5: My Six-Word Statement on Motivation

_____ _____ _____ _____ _____ _____

Focus on Word Study

Root: *hydro*
Meaning: _____
Common Words That Contain the Root:

1.

2.

3.

My Wacky Word

_____

_____

_____

_____

Write-On Sheet

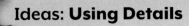

Ideas: Using Details

Preview

A Product Designer

Answer the questions below, on your own or with a partner.

1. Product designers plan and develop products that fulfill a need and improve users' lives. What do you think is the most interesting part of the job? Most challenging?

   _____

   _____

   _____

   _____

2. What do you think a product designer does first when they begin to plan and develop their product idea?

   _____

   _____

   _____

   _____

3. What is a product you started to use recently? What attracted you to the product?

   _____

   _____

   _____

   _____

Bonus: Look up on the Internet what a product designer does. Write your findings on index cards and share them with a classmate.

Slogans That Motivate

Hint: "Be kind, you bonehead!" is *not* a good slogan.

With a partner, come up with three slogans that will motivate middle school students to do something kind for another person.

Slogan 1: _____

_____

Slogan 2: _____

_____

Slogan 3: _____

_____

Now, choose one of your slogans and plan a poster. Think "details"!

1. Slogan for my poster: _____

_____

_____

_____

2. Visual images and design elements: _____

_____

_____

_____

3. Quotations and/or other text features I will include: _____

_____

_____

_____

- Creating the Lead
- Using Sequence Words and Transition Words
- Structuring the Body
- **Ending With a Sense of Resolution** ·············

Focus Mode: Persuasive
Theme: Motivation

Organization

Organization is about how your idea unfolds from beginning to end—how you structure and arrange your details. An organized piece of writing begins engagingly, moves along logically, and ends satisfyingly. You give readers the right amount of information at the right moments. When your organization is working, following the idea is effortless.

Ending With a Sense of Resolution

The ending is your last contact with readers—your opportunity to make them say *ah, yes,* not *huh?!* A good ending ties up the loose ends and answers any remaining questions. It sums up your thinking in a natural, thoughtful, and convincing way, and leaves readers with a sense of closure.

Or-ga-nize!
Or-ga-nize!
Go, Writers, go!

Organization

HOME

00:01

GUEST

PERIOD 4

• BONUS

POSS •

BONUS

FOULS

SHOT CLOCK

:17

FOULS

How is creating a great ending in a piece of writing like winning a sporting event?

Endings That Nail It

Here are some techniques to wrap up your writing and make it feel finished. You might use one technique in your piece, or combine two or more for maximum impact.

1. Sum It Up

Summarize important points in your piece or offer the reader a moral or a lesson . . . but **don't** end with:

Those are the three reasons why, or *They all lived happily ever after.*

2. Look Back

Refer back to your lead or to questions that you posed in your piece; answer any unanswered questions . . . but **don't** end with:

That's all I know about armadillos, or *Read about armadillos online if you want to know more.*

3. Use the Words of Others

Include a thought-provoking quotation, proverb, or adage that reinforces your main idea . . . but **don't** end with clichés such as:

Keep working because a rolling stone gathers no moss, or *When in Rome, do as the Romans.*

4. Inspire Action

Leave the reader with a question to ponder or challenge to embrace . . . but **don't** end with a predictable question or comment like:

Do you know more about electricity now? I know I do, or *You can change the world.*

5. Try a Literary Technique

Use alliteration, a simile or metaphor, a touch of irony, or powerful imagery . . . but **don't** end with a statement that tries too hard:

Ancient Egyptians had a hard life, as hard as nails and steel.

6. Delight the Reader

Treat the reader to a surprise, a laugh, a profound thought, an encouraging message, or an unusual insight . . . in other words—unless you're a movie producer—**never** end with:

The End

R.A.F.T.S. 17

There's a new restaurant opening up called The Mustard Shack and the whole town's been dying to try it. Because your best friend is a server there, you were able to get in on opening night and had a *very* distinctive experience. You can't wait to tell others exactly how it went (good or bad) and decide to post an online review in which you detail your trip and end with a sense of resolution you hope will convince other diners of the pros and/or cons of visiting this eatery.

Role: diner at The Mustard Shack
Audience: restaurant goers
Format: online restaurant review
Topic: food and service at The Mustard Shack
Strong Verbs: post, detail, convince

Write your review on a separate sheet of paper. Before you begin to write, jot down some details you might include:

Think About

- Have I wrapped up all the loose ends?
- Have I ended at the best place?
- Do I have an ending that makes my writing feel finished?
- Did I leave the reader with something to think about?

Jump Start Sheet

Days 1 and 3: My Unit Project To-Do List

- _____
- _____
- _____
- _____

Day 5: My Six-Word Statement on Motivation

_____ _____ _____ _____ _____ _____

Focus on Grammar and Usage

Review your writing, find sentences in which you've used verb tenses incorrectly, and revise two of those sentences here.

1. _____

   _____

   _____

   _____

2. _____

   _____

   _____

   _____

Write-On Sheet

Preview

Diane Swanson, author of *Burp! The Most Interesting Book You'll Ever Read About Eating*

Answer the questions below on your own or with a partner.

1. Diane Swanson says that young people and a love of nature inspire her as a writer. What kinds of books would you expect her to write?

   _____

   _____

2. One tip Swanson always gives young writers is to write about what excites them. What is it about writing on topics you like that makes the writing easier for you?

   _____

   _____

3. Swanson sought the insights of nutritionists and scientists when she wrote *Burp!* Why is talking to experts important?

   _____

   _____

4. One of Swanson's other books is *Nibbling on Einstein's Brain: The Good, the Bad, and the Bogus in Science.* What is a question you'd hope would be answered in that book?

   _____

   _____

Bonus: Find one or two more facts about Diane Swanson on the Internet. Share them with a classmate.

Catching Zzzz's

> The book is called *Snooze!* As its writer, you'd better make sure it isn't one.

Imagine you've been asked to write a book on sleep called *Snooze!* With a partner, plan a section to persuade readers to get enough sleep by describing how getting too little sleep affects the mind and body. List three negative effects (for example, "You nod off in class.") and three consequences for each effect (for example, "no learning," "poor grades," "embarrassing snoring").

Topic: the negative effects of too little sleep

Effect 1:

Effect 2:

Effect 3:

Consequences

1. _____
2. _____
3. _____

1. _____
2. _____
3. _____

1. _____
2. _____
3. _____

Work with your partner to write the lead and body of your section on a separate sheet. When you finish, on your own, draft the ending below. Share the draft with your partner and collaborate on the final ending.

_____

_____

_____

_____

- Establishing a Tone
- Conveying the Purpose
- Creating a Connection to the Audience
- **Taking Risks to Create Voice** ··················

Focus Mode: Persuasive
Theme: Motivation

Voice

Voice is the energy and attitude of a piece of writing. In fiction, voice can take on almost any tone, from humorous or hopeful to serious or somber. In nonfiction, it is often compelling, authoritative, and knowledgeable. You arrive at the right voice for a piece by thinking deeply about your purpose and your audience for it. You "speak" in a way that connects to your audience.

Taking Risks to Create Voice

> My eyeballs are connected to my body by threads. Everything I do is a risk.

If you want to break away from bland, "voice-less" writing, you'll have to take some risks. That means you may have to tackle topics that are new to you. You may have to use words and phrases you've never used before. This may feel uncomfortable at first. But it will become natural with practice. You'll find that taking risks leads to writing that is truly your own.

How is taking risks to create voice in writing like wearing whatever clothes strike your fancy?

It's a Risky Business

When you take risks to create voice in writing, you come up with a fresh take on your topic. You get the reader's attention by coming up with fresh and original ways to express your ideas. As you write, experiment with these risk-taking techniques.

1. **Find new ways to say familiar things.**

   Ditch everyday language for words and phrases that make your writing original.

   Example: *He was a Sasquatch of a man, with thick limbs and a thatch of wild red hair.*

2. **Use satire to poke fun at a situation.**

   Make room for satire, a literary form in which the writer uses irony, sarcasm, and even ridicule to make a point—and make the reader chuckle.

   Example: *How do I like sharing a room with my baby brother? Oh, about as much as I'd like a steady diet of liver and onions.*

3. **Don't be afraid to let your feelings show.**

   Let your writing reflect how you feel. Express your passions and opinions about your subject.

   Example: *Many people say that composting is difficult and messy. That's simply ridiculous! It doesn't take a degree in biology to maintain a compost pile. And all that free organic fertilizer is pure gold to backyard gardeners.*

4. **Think outside the box. Write from a different point of view.**

   Give animals or inanimate objects a human voice.

   Example: *Well, look who gets to drive me today! Hey, fella! Do your parents know you've got the car keys? Wait a minute! Not so fast! Before we go anywhere, just put on that seat belt. That's right. Now take it slow down the driveway. Not THAT slow—we need to get there before next year!*

R.A.F.T.S. 18

You are uncomfortable. You're covered in mold. You stink. And you're not happy about it. You are a plastic food container that was used for a teenager's lunch . . . and then forgotten in his or her locker. Write a speech that you will deliver to the negligent teen, urging him or her to find you and wash you up as soon as possible.

Role: plastic food container with old leftovers
Audience: the teenager who last used you
Format: speech
Topic: need to be cleaned
Strong Verbs: deliver, urge

Write your speech on a separate sheet of paper. Before you begin to write, jot down some details you might include.

Think About

- Have I used words that are not ordinary?
- Is my writing interesting, fresh, and original?
- Have I tried to make my writing sound like me?
- Have I tried something different from what I've done before?

Voice: Taking Risks to Create Voice

Jump Start **Sheet**

Days 1 and 3: My Unit Project To-Do List

- _____

- _____

- _____

- _____

Day 5: My Six-Word Statement on Motivation:

_____ _____ _____ _____ _____ _____

Focus on Word Study

Root: *rupt*
Meaning: _____
Common Words That Contain the Root:

1.

2.

3.

My Wacky Word

_____

_____

_____

_____

Write-On Sheet

Preview

Nick Bruel, author of *Bad Kitty Gets a Bath*

Answer the questions below, on your own or with a partner.

1. Ever since elementary school, Nick Bruel has enjoyed writing and illustrating stories. What are the advantages of creating both words and pictures?

   _____

   _____

2. When he was young, Bruel read lots of comic books. As an adult, he worked in a children's bookstore. How might both of these activities have influenced his work as an author?

   _____

   _____

3. Even though Bruel's comical character Bad Kitty tries to be good, she is always getting into trouble. What other characters from books or comics have this same problem?

   _____

   _____

4. Bruel has written a series of books featuring Bad Kitty. Name a book series you've enjoyed reading.

   _____

   _____

Bonus: On the Internet, find one or two more facts about Nick Bruel. Share them with a classmate.

Bad Kitty's Top Ten Ways to Avoid a Bath

Think of ten suggestions Bad Kitty might make to other cats for avoiding the dreaded "human bath" experience. List Bad Kitty's pieces of advice here, from least (#10) to most (#1) persuasive. Be sure to take some risks by offering suggestions the average cat wouldn't already know.

Start that list. What's the matter, kitty got your tongue?

Start with a "light" touch . . .

10. _____

9. _____

8. _____

7. _____

6. _____

5. _____

4. _____

3. _____

2. _____

If all else fails, pull out all the stops and . . .

1. _____

Persuasive Publishing Checklist

Think you are ready to go public with your persuasive unit project? Use this form to make sure you've covered all the writing bases.

Okay, okay . . . you've convinced me. Can we move on now?

I remembered to

☐ state my position on the topic clearly and stick with it.

☐ offer good, sound reasoning that the reader can relate to easily.

☐ provide solid facts, opinions, and examples that are based on reliable, objective sources.

☐ expose weaknesses in other positions.

☐ develop my argument using solid reasoning from beginning to end.

☐ use a compelling, confident voice to add credibility.

☐ explain any unusual words, phrases, or concepts.

☐ read my piece aloud to check how it will sound to the reader.

☐ proofread my piece carefully and clean up problems with conventions.

The purpose of my piece is

_____

The most critical point I make is

_____

What I hope readers will take away from my piece is

_____

_____

All

Focus Mode: Narrative

Since the start of human history, people have been telling stories to make sense of the world. When you write in the narrative mode, you tell a story—either a made-up one (fiction) or a real one (nonfiction). Your stories should include characters, a setting, a timeline, and a problem and its solution. Along the way, they may include a surprise or two. And they should always capture your reader's interest and hang on to it, right to the end.

- Applying Strong Verbs
- Selecting Striking Words and Phrases
- Using Specific and Accurate Words
- **Choosing Words That Deepen Meaning** ·

Focus Mode: Narrative
Theme: Imagination

Word Choice

Words are the building blocks of writing. Well-chosen words bring your ideas into focus. They create images, spark the imagination, and grab the reader's attention. Word choice is verbal alchemy; it's how writers transform the ordinary into the extraordinary. Choose words that move, enlighten, and inspire.

Choosing Words That Deepen Meaning

Climbing mountains is tiring, draining, exhausting, wearying, fatiguing . . .

Word Choice

Good writers know that the first words that come to mind are rarely the ones they end up using. They take time to think about words and move them around in their drafts. Replacing dull, common words with exciting, original ones helps you express exactly what you want to say in your writing.

How is snapping a terrific photo like choosing words that deepen meaning?

Word Choice: **Choosing Words That Deepen Meaning**

Going Deep!

Here are four techniques to help you find the words you're looking for.

1. **Consider the Context**

   One word may work best in one situation, and a synonym for it may work best in another. For example, use the word *chilly* if you feel just a little bit cold and *frigid* when you are in the Arctic.

2. **Try for a Fresh Image**

   Don't settle for words and phrases that are really familiar or clichéd, such as *terrifying* or *made my blood run cold*, to describe something scary. Instead, take the time to find a fresher word or phrase such as *petrifying* or *could've scared the stripes off a zebra*.

3. **Avoid the Obvious**

   Try two, three, or as many as necessary until you get the right word. For example, which fits better: *The heat and humidity were terrible* or *It was so hot and humid, chickens were laying hard-boiled eggs*?

4. **Use Analogies**

   Try making a comparison between two unlike people, places, or things to make your point clearly and forcefully. For example, instead of saying, *He was so inconsiderate*, you could say, *He was as considerate as a grizzly bear on a rampage*.

R.A.F.T.S. 19

You're a farmer, and this year you've grown a pumpkin the size of a small house—surely a grand prize-winner at the Hootabloota County Fair. But, you have two hours to get there and you're trapped in your barn . . . by your own farm animals! Tired of being neglected in favor of the pumpkin, the animals have rebelled, corralling you in the barn with only your cell phone. Place a 911 call explaining what has happened. Relate the events in meaningful detail, using words that describe what happened and how you feel about it. Be sure to impress upon the dispatcher how important the fair is to your business so that he or she will understand the need to act quickly.

Role: a farmer
Audience: 911 dispatcher
Format: telephone call
Topic: trapped in the barn by an angry (smelly) mob
Strong Verbs: explain, relate, describe

Write a transcript of your call on a separate sheet of paper. Before you begin to write, jot down some details you might include.

Think About

- Did I choose words that show I really thought about them?
- Have I tried to use words without repeating myself?
- Do my words capture the reader's imagination?
- Have I found the best way to express myself?

Word Choice: **Choosing Words That Deepen Meaning**

Jump Start Sheet

Days 1 and 3: My Unit Project To-Do List

- _____
- _____
- _____
- _____

Day 5: My Six-Word Statement on Imagination

_____ _____ _____ _____ _____ _____

Focus on Grammar and Usage

Review your writing, find sentences in which you've used verbs and predicate adjectives incorrectly. Revise two of those sentences here.

1. _____

   _____

   _____

   _____

2. _____

   _____

   _____

   _____

Write-On Sheet

Word Choice: **Choosing Words That Deepen Meaning**

Preview

A Product Copywriter

Answer the questions below on your own or with a partner.

1. A product copywriter writes the text that appears on product packaging. What information do you look for on the packaging of your favorite products, such as cereal?

_____

_____

_____

_____

2. What do you think are the purposes of package copy?

_____

_____

_____

_____

3. Why do you think product copywriters need to be careful about the words and phrases they choose?

_____

_____

_____

_____

Bonus: Look up on the Internet what a product copywriter does. Write your findings on note cards and share them with a classmate.

Delicious and Delectable

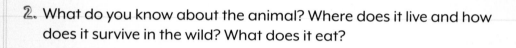

I had a pet sneaker, but it kept running away.

Think of an unusual pet—go for something you rarely hear about. Then answer these questions to plan the packaging for a treat that will appeal to that pet.

1. What unusual pet did you choose?

_____

2. What do you know about the animal? Where does it live and how does it survive in the wild? What does it eat?

_____

_____

3. What is your treat made from? How do you know it is healthy for the animal?

_____

_____

4. What will your treat look like? Describe its size, color, and shape.

_____

_____

5. What is its product name? What is its parent company's name?

_____

_____

On a separate sheet of paper, create a design for your packaging. Below the design, draft the copy (a narrative testimonial from a satisfied customer). Be sure to entice potential buyers, using information from this planning sheet. Choose "just right" words to deepen meaning.

- Crafting Well-Built Sentences
- Varying Sentence Types
- Capturing Smooth and Rhythmic Flow
- **Breaking the "Rules" to Create Fluency** ·····························

**Focus Mode: Narrative
Theme: Imagination**

Sentence Fluency

Writing may seem like a silent act, but it isn't. When you read your drafts, listen for passages that sound smooth and rhythmic . . . and passages that don't. From there, revise. By doing that, you'll create sentence fluency—the music of language that makes your writing sound as good as it looks.

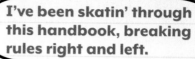

I've been skatin' through this handbook, breaking rules right and left.

Breaking the "Rules" to Create Fluency

Following grammar rules makes your writing understandable, but not always engaging. Sometimes you have to break the rules to energize your writing. Use sentence fragments to make a point. Or start a sentence or two with a conjunction. Write the way you talk. Surprise your reader—unleash your creativity.

Sentence Fluency

How is defying the laws of gravity like breaking the rules of English in writing?

Breaking the "Rules": What Works?

Breaking these four rules thoughtfully can help make your writing fluent to the reader's ear.

1. **Never use sentence fragments.**

   Example: *Eating everything in sight. That was his desire after five days without food. To eat nonstop. To eat anything edible.*

   So why would a writer use sentence fragments? Fragments can create welcome pauses in writing and can help you emphasize important points. Just be sure to use them sparingly and purposefully.

2. **Never repeat words and phrases.**

   Example: *I walked outside. It was hot. It was very hot. It was so hot, I had to jump in the water—immediately.*

   Why might a writer decide to repeat words and phrases? Repetition can give your writing a rhythmic sound and heighten the impact of a critical message.

3. **Never start a sentence with a conjunction.**

   Example: *And so it went, until the bell rang and we left for home.*

   Why start a sentence with a conjunction? A conjunction can give your writing a conversational tone and, therefore, help you connect to your reader. A conjunction also lets the reader know immediately whether you're continuing a thought or switching gears.

4. **Never use grammatically incorrect dialogue or slang.**

   Example: *"I can't never do nothing right," Ella grumbled in discouragement. "It just don't work out the way I want it to."*

   So why would a writer use grammatically incorrect dialogue or slang? To add dimension to characters and make them more believable. But if you decide to break this rule, remember to base it on who your characters are, where they come from, and what matters to them.

R.A.F.T.S. 20

You are a robot who has been purchased by a family to run their household. Since you don't need sleep, you like to spend your downtime writing articles for *Bionic 8.0*, the e-zine all sophisticated robots e-read. Today you've decided to relate all the crazy things that happened when you tried out a new dog-walking hand attachment and it went haywire. Remember to be imaginative as you narrate what happened: you're a robot and your programming includes all the rules of English—and how to break them.

Role: robot
Audience: your fellow robots
Format: magazine article
Topic: day spent with a dog-walking hand attachment gone haywire
Strong Verbs: relate, narrate, be creative

Write your article on a separate sheet of paper. Before you begin to write, jot down some details you might include.

Think About

- Did I use fragments with style and purpose?
- Do I begin a sentence informally to create a conversational tone?
- Does my dialogue sound authentic?
- Did I try weaving in exclamations and single words to add emphasis?

Jump Start Sheet

Days 1 and 3: My Unit Project To-Do List

- _____
- _____
- _____
- _____

Day 5: My Six-Word Statement on Imagination

_____ _____ _____ _____ _____ _____

Focus on Word Study

Root: _mob_
Meaning: _____

Common Words That Contain the Root:

1.

2.

3.

My Wacky Word

_____

_____

_____

_____

Write-On Sheet

Sentence Fluency: **Breaking the "Rules" to Create Fluency**

Preview

Rodman Philbrick, author of
The Mostly True Adventures of Homer P. Figg

Answer the questions below, on your own or with a partner.

1. Before writing his many successful published novels, Rodman Philbrick wrote lots of stories that have never been published. What does this say about his desire and drive to be a writer?

   _____

   _____

   _____

2. Rodman says that his characters are based on people he knows, but that he makes up his plots. What person do you know who would make a good character in a novel?

   _____

   _____

   _____

3. Homer P. Figg's adventures take place during the Civil War. How can a writer from the present make characters from the past seem believable and interesting to today's readers?

   _____

   _____

   _____

Bonus: On the Internet, look up books by Rodman Philbrick. On a note card, write the titles of several books. Share with a classmate what you find and tell him or her which you'd most like to read and why.

It Happened That Night

I think Bob asks for a throat lozenge because he's a little "horse."

What happens to Homer and his horse, Bob, when they ride off into the darkness? Use the top section to plan your story. Then write a paragraph-length version that follows the rules of standard English and one that breaks them. If necessary, use a separate sheet of paper.

Sentence Fluency

Characters: _____

Setting: _____

Plot: _____

Follows rules of standard English:

_____

_____

_____

_____

_____

Breaks rules of standard English:

_____

_____

_____

_____

- Ideas
- Organization
- Voice
- Word Choice
- Sentence Fluency
- Conventions
- Presentation

Focus Mode:
Narrative

Theme:
Imagination

All Traits

Whether you're writing a persuasive piece to lobby for an overnight school trip, an expository piece describing sun dogs, or a narrative piece telling the story of a moose that wandered into your yard, you must be skilled in all the traits in order to grab and hold your reader's attention.

Putting the Traits Together

All year, you have been reading your writing closely and breaking it down, trait by trait. Working with the traits like this has helped you develop new writing skills. Let's put everything you've learned out on the table this week and see how much you've improved.

What do a jigsaw puzzle and a piece of writing have in common?

The Traits Team

In a strong piece of writing, the revision traits work together as a team, each playing a very important position.

Ideas: the content of the piece

Organization: the internal structure of the piece

Voice: the tone of the piece

Word Choice: the specific vocabulary the writer uses to convey meaning

Sentence Fluency: the way the text looks and sounds as it flows through the piece

Conventions: the mechanical correctness of the piece

Presentation: the physical appearance of the piece

Think about these seven traits and then read the passage below. Look for evidence of each trait at work.

Careful, It Stings!

"Ouch!"

"What do you mean, 'Ouch!'?" Dad said, as he dabbed my cut with iodine.

"What do you mean, 'What do you mean?' That stuff stings. Have you never had iodine patted into a fresh cut in your long, long, long life?"

"I think two 'longs' will do," he smirked. "I'm a mere forty-eight. That hardly qualifies me for Social Security." He bent his aging eyes closer to the cut as he wiped, so that he could see what he was doing without his glasses. (Didn't want to embarrass himself in front of his youngest child—me—who he knew would pester him about it.) "So tell me again how you managed to cut yourself opening a bag of wheat crackers?"

"I told you," I said, irritated. "You know how sometimes the bag won't open even when you pull and pull? Whatever. So I got scissors, but then I got a text, so I multitasked, you know to read it, while I tried to cut the bag open, and . . ." I sighed loudly. "Oh, never mind."

It sounded too silly when I described it aloud.

R.A.F.T.S. 21

Whoa! You're the first historian chosen to take the sparkly, shiny, newly invented time machine out for a spin. You've just returned from your maiden voyage and are itching to tell all about your trip—what you've witnessed boggles the imagination. Write a travel narrative that does just that: describe what the trip was like, when and where you went, whom you saw, what you did. Since your narrative will probably be published for the world to see, you'll want to use all of the traits to their fullest potential in this piece. Be sure to identify the historical era and provide any historical context needed.

Role: historian
Audience: the world
Format: historical (time-travel) narrative
Topic: a historical era or event of your choice
Strong Verbs: describe, identify

Write your travel narrative on a separate sheet of paper. Before you begin to write, jot down some details you might include.

Think About

- Does my writing show that I understand my topic?

- Are my details in the best possible order?

- Can the reader tell I care about this idea?

- Have I painted a picture with words?

- Does my writing sound good when read aloud?

Jump Start Sheet

Days 1 and 3: My Unit Project To-Do List

- _____
- _____
- _____
- _____

Day 5: My Six-Word Statement on Imagination

_____ _____ _____ _____ _____ _____

Focus on Grammar and Usage

Review your writing and find sentences in which you've used the wrong form of an irregular verb or a homophone. Revise two of those sentences here.

1. _____
   _____
   _____
   _____

2. _____
   _____
   _____
   _____

Write-On Sheet

Preview

Barbara Kerley, author of
Greetings From Planet Earth

Answer the questions below, on your own or with a partner.

1. After college, Barbara Kerley spent two years as a Peace Corps volunteer in Nepal. How could travel help a writer find ideas?

   _____

   _____

   _____

2. Kerley writes biographies as well as fiction. What skills as a biographer might help her write fiction? What skills as a fiction writer help her write biographies?

   _____

   _____

   _____

3. In *Greetings From Planet Earth*, the main character, Theo, and his class choose images of humanity to send into space to help aliens understand earthlings. What images of humanity would you send?

   _____

   _____

   _____

Bonus: Look on the Internet for more about Barbara Kerley. Write down on a note card an interesting fact you discover or the name of a book you might like to read. Share with a classmate what you find.

Who Are We?

In *Greetings From Planet Earth*, teacher Mr. Meyer assigns a project based on the question, "What would someone from another planet need to know to understand us?" Use the chart below to plan your answer to that question.

Trait	Notes
Ideas Think about your topic, focus, and the details to include.	
Organization Think about possible structures, leads, and maybe even endings.	
Voice Think about your purpose, audience, and appropriate tones.	
Word Choice Think about strong verbs, striking words, specific and accurate words, and words that deepen meaning.	
Sentence Fluency Think about writing sentences of different types and lengths to create a smooth and rhythmic flow.	
Conventions Think about spelling, capitalizing, and punctuating well. Follow the rules of English—or break them for good reasons.	

Put your ideas together. On a separate sheet of paper, answer the question: "What would someone from another planet need to know to understand us?"

Narrative Publishing Checklist

Think you are ready to go public with your narrative unit project? Use this form to make sure you've covered all the writing bases.

Check. Check. Check. Uh oh! Check.

I remembered to

☐ present a clear, well-developed story line.

☐ include fascinating characters that grow and change over time.

☐ convey a time and setting that make sense for the story.

☐ entertain, surprise, and challenge the reader.

☐ develop the story chronologically or take a risk to try a structure that also helps the reader follow the story easily.

☐ use an active voice to engage the reader.

☐ choose words that fit the characters, time, and place.

☐ read my piece aloud to check for places where I should speed up or slow down.

☐ proofread my piece carefully and clean up problems with conventions.

The purpose of my piece is

_____

My favorite part is

_____

What I hope readers will find most memorable about my piece is

_____

Week

1

Looking Back on
Myself as a Writer

Week

2

Writing as Experts

Week

3

Fun Writing-Related
Activities

Week

4

More Writing-Related
Activities

Wrapping Up the Year

As the writing year draws to a close, let's
look back at what you've learned about
writing and how the traits have helped
you improve. We'll stop to enjoy what
you've written, look ahead to next year,
and while we're at it, have some fun.

The beginning of the school year . . . that was a while back, wasn't it? To get from there to here, you've spent lots of time writing and learning about writing. Now it's time to wrap up the writing year. This week, you will

1 contribute to a class exhibit about writing. You'll combine written text and visuals to create a poster.

2 write a letter introducing yourself to next year's writing teacher. You'll include details about how you've grown as a writer, and what you still need to work on.

Design Studio

Use this page to sketch your ideal poster about writing. When you've finished, share it with your fellow group members and use everyone's ideas to create the final product, including text.

Viewer's Notes

As you take in the exhibit, write notes about the posters.

Something a group did that works especially well:

_____

_____

_____

 A terrific design idea:

_____

_____

_____

Examples of good writing:

_____

_____

_____

The poster (other than ours) that communicates the message most effectively:

_____

_____

_____

_____

Me, the Writer

Fill in this sheet to gather information to include in your letter to next year's teacher.

1. Something I wrote this year that shows how much I've learned as a writer:

   _____

   _____

   _____

2. Two key qualities that helped me become a better writer:

   _____

   _____

   _____

3. Two key qualities I want to work on next year:

   _____

   _____

   _____

4. A statement about the importance of writing in my life:

   _____

   _____

   _____

Writing as Experts

Think about all the writing you did this year—and all you've learned about writing from your efforts. It's time to take a close look at just how much you've grown, and from there, use your expertise to help next year's entering class. This week, you will

1 write a paper in the same mode and on the same general topic as your beginning-of-year benchmark paper. You'll reread the original and compare the two pieces to see what you've learned.

2 write "Dos and Don'ts for Surviving Writing Class" for incoming sixth graders.

3 clean out your writing folder.

Benchmark Paper Planning Page

Write the topic and mode of your beginning-of-year paper. Then use the space below to plan a new paper on the same topic and in the same mode. Feel free to make lists of key points, write guiding questions, create a graphic organizer, or do anything else that will help you organize your thoughts. When your brain says, "Enough planning!" start writing your draft on a separate sheet of paper.

Topic: _____   Mode: _____

Writing as Experts

Revision and Editing Reminders

Revising and editing can take a lot of time, so let's keep the instructions simple.

1. **Reread your draft and think about**
   - adding and deleting information and making details specific and accurate.
   - checking the beginning and ending to make sure they work well.
   - using a tone that is appropriate for your audience and captures the right amount of energy.
   - eliminating repetitive words and phrases, and replacing them with more original ones.
   - creating smooth and rhythmic flow by varying sentence beginnings, lengths, and types.

2. **Go ahead and revise your draft.**

3. **Now look at your piece with an editor's eye by**
   - checking spelling.
   - using correct punctuation.
   - finding the right places to capitalize.
   - applying grammar and usage rules.

4. **Create a final piece for the reader.**

Pass It Along: The Dos and Don'ts of Writing Class

Brainstorm with a partner a hefty list of tips for surviving writing class, based on what you've learned this year.

Dos

Don'ts

Choose your top three "Dos" and top three "Don'ts," and write them out on a separate sheet of paper. It's okay to be funny, as long as each tip is honest and helpful.

Fun Writing-Related Activities

The end of the year is approaching, and you've done a lot of writing since it began. When you stop to think about it, you'll realize that what you've learned this year will last you the rest of your life—because writing is an essential skill, no matter where you go or what you do.

This week, the scale tips to the "fun" side of writing, with group activities that allow you to show what you know!

Bringing a Superhero to Life

Decide which trait is your hero's specialty. Then use the chart to help define the character and map out the mission to save good writing.

Superhero of the _____ Trait

Its Name
Its Superpower
Its Archenemy
How It Rescues Writing

More Writing-Related Activities

Now it's definitely time to enter the no-assignment zone, kick back, and have some fun. You'll also want to review your remaining writing and take home the pieces that mean the most to you, so that you can read them in years to come. And don't forget to give your teacher a hand in taking down bulletin boards, cleaning up the classroom, and storing materials for next year's class. From there, say so long to your classmates—and thanks for a great year of writing!

Picture Book Design

A picture book about the traits? Why not! Plan a picture book for young children by filling in the chart below. Then use your notes to create the book on separate sheets of paper.

Trait	Thoughts About the Text	Thoughts About the Illustrations
Ideas		
Organization		
Voice		
Word Choice		
Sentence Fluency		
Conventions		
Presentation		

Ideas

the content of the piece—its central message and the details that support that message

6 EXPERT

HIGH

My topic is well developed and focused. My piece contains specific, interesting, and accurate details, and new thinking about this topic.

- I have a clear central theme or a simple, original story line.
- I've narrowed my theme or story line to create a focused piece that is a pleasure to read.
- I've included original information to support my main idea.
- I've included specific, interesting, and accurate details that will create pictures in the reader's mind.

5 WELL DONE

4 ALMOST THERE

MIDDLE

My piece includes many general observations about the topic, but lacks focus and clear, accurate details. I need to elaborate.

- I've stayed on the topic, but my theme or story line is too broad.
- I haven't dug into the topic in a logical, focused way.
- My unique perspective on this topic is not coming through as clearly as it could.
- The reader may have questions after reading this piece because my details leave some questions unanswered.

3 MAKING STRIDES

2 ON MY WAY

LOW

I'm still thinking about the theme or story line for this piece. So far, I've only explored possibilities.

- I've jotted down some ideas for topics, but it's a hodgepodge.
- Nothing in particular stands out as important in my piece.
- I have not written much. I may have only restated the assignment.
- My details are thin and need to be checked for accuracy.

1 GETTING STARTED

Organization

the internal structure of the piece—the thread of logic, the pattern of meaning

6 EXPERT

HIGH

My details unfold in a logical order. The structure makes reading my piece a breeze.

- My beginning grabs the reader's attention.
- I've used sequence and transition words to guide the reader.
- All of my details fit together logically and move along smoothly.
- My ending gives the reader a sense of closure and something to think about.

5 WELL DONE

4 ALMOST THERE

MIDDLE

My piece's organization is pretty basic and predictable. I have the three essential ingredients, a beginning, middle, and end, but that's about it.

- My beginning is clear, but unoriginal. I've used a technique that writers use all too often.
- I've used simple sequence and transition words that stand out too much.
- Details need to be added or moved around to create a more logical flow of ideas.
- My ending needs work; it's pretty canned.

3 MAKING STRIDES

2 ON MY WAY

LOW

My piece doesn't make much sense because I haven't figured out a way to organize it. The details are jumbled together at this point.

- My beginning doesn't indicate where I'm going or why I'm going there.
- I have not grouped ideas or connected them using sequence and transition words.
- With no sense of order, it will be a challenge for the reader to sort out how the details relate.
- I haven't figured out how to end this piece.

1 GETTING STARTED

Voice

the tone of the piece—the personal stamp of the writer—which is achieved through an understanding of purpose and audience

HIGH

6 EXPERT

I've come up with my own "take" on the topic. I had my audience and purpose clearly in mind as I wrote and presented my ideas in an original way.

- My piece is expressive, which shows how much I care about my topic.
- The purpose for this piece is clear, and I've used a tone that suits that purpose.
- There is no doubt in my mind that the reader will understand how I think and feel about my topic.
- I've expressed myself in some new, original ways.

5 WELL DONE

MIDDLE

4 ALMOST THERE

My feelings about the topic come across as uninspired and predictable. The piece is not all that expressive, nor does it reveal a commitment to the topic.

- In a few places, my authentic voice comes through, but only in a few.
- My purpose for writing this piece is unclear to me, so the tone feels "off."
- I've made little effort to connect with the reader; I'm playing it safe.
- This piece sounds like lots of others on this topic. It's not very original.

3 MAKING STRIDES

2 ON MY WAY

LOW

I haven't thought at all about my purpose or audience for the piece and, therefore, my voice falls flat. I'm pretty indifferent to the topic and it shows.

- I've put no energy into this piece.
- My purpose for writing this piece is a mystery to me, so I'm casting about aimlessly.
- Since my topic isn't interesting to me, chances are my piece won't be interesting to the reader. I haven't thought about my audience.
- I have taken no risks. There is no evidence that I find this topic interesting or care about it at all.

1 GETTING STARTED

Word Choice

the specific vocabulary you use to convey meaning and enlighten the reader

HIGH

6 EXPERT

The words and phrases I've selected are accurate, specific, and natural-sounding. My piece conveys precisely what I want to say, because of my powerful vocabulary.

- My piece contains strong verbs that bring it alive.
- I stretched by using the perfect words and phrases to convey my ideas.
- I've used content words and phrases with accuracy and precision.
- I've picked the best words and phrases, not just the first ones that came to mind.

5 WELL DONE

4 ALMOST THERE

MIDDLE

My words and phrases make sense but aren't very accurate, specific, or natural-sounding. The reader won't have trouble understanding them. However, he or she may find them uninspiring.

- I've used passive voice. I should rethink passages that contain passive voice and add "action words."
- I haven't come up with extraordinary ways to say ordinary things.
- My content words and phrases are accurate but general. I might have overused jargon. I need to choose words that are more precise.
- I need to revise this piece by replacing its weak words and phrases with strong ones.

3 MAKING STRIDES

2 ON MY WAY

LOW

My words and phrases are so unclear, the reader may wind up more confused than entertained, informed, or persuaded. I need to expand my vocabulary to improve this piece.

- My verbs are not strong. Passive voice permeates this piece.
- I've used bland words and phrases throughout—or the same words and phrases over and over.
- My content words are neither specific nor accurate enough to make the meaning clear.
- My words and phrases are not working; they distract the reader rather than guide him or her.

1 GETTING STARTED

Sentence Fluency

the way the text looks and sounds as it flows through the piece

HIGH

6 EXPERT

My piece is strong because I've written a variety of well-built sentences. I've woven those sentences together to create a smooth-sounding piece.

- I've constructed and connected my sentences for maximum impact.
- I've varied my sentence lengths and types—short and long, simple and complex.
- When I read my piece aloud, it is pleasing to my ear.
- I've broken grammar rules intentionally at points to create impact and interest.

5 WELL DONE

4 ALMOST THERE

MIDDLE

Although my sentences lack variety or creativity, most of them are grammatically correct. Some of them are smooth, while others are choppy and awkward.

- I've written solid shorter sentences. Now I need to try some longer ones.
- I've created different kinds of sentences, but the result is uneven.
- When I read my piece aloud, I stumble in a few places.
- Any sentences that break grammar rules are accidental and don't work well.

3 MAKING STRIDES

2 ON MY WAY

LOW

My sentences are choppy, incomplete, or rambling. I need to revise my piece extensively to make it more readable.

- Many of my sentences don't work because they're poorly constructed.
- I've used the same sentence lengths and types over and over again.
- When I read my piece aloud, I stumble in many places.
- If I've broken grammar rules, it's not for stylistic reasons—it's because I may not understand those rules.

1 GETTING STARTED

Conventions

the mechanical correctness of the piece, which helps guide the reader through the text

6 EXPERT

HIGH

My piece proves I can use a range of conventions with skill and creativity. It is ready for its intended audience.

- My spelling is strong. I've spelled all or nearly all the words accurately.

- I've used punctuation creatively and correctly and have begun new paragraphs in the right places.

- I've used capital letters correctly throughout my piece, even in tricky places.

- I've taken care to apply standard English grammar and usage.

5 WELL DONE

4 ALMOST THERE

MIDDLE

My writing still needs editing to correct problems in one or more conventions. I've stuck to the basics and haven't tried challenging conventions.

- I've misspelled words that I use all the time, as well as complex words that I don't use as often.

- My punctuation is basically strong, but I should review it one more time. I indented some of the paragraphs, but not all of them.

- I've correctly used capital letters in obvious places (such as the word *I*) but not in others.

- Even though my grammar and usage are not 100 percent correct, my audience should be able to read my piece.

3 MAKING STRIDES

2 ON MY WAY

LOW

The problems I'm having with conventions make this piece challenging to read, even for me! I've got lots of work to do before it's ready for its intended audience.

- Extensive spelling errors make my piece difficult to read and understand.

- I haven't punctuated or paragraphed the piece well, which makes it difficult for the reader to understand or enjoy my writing.

- My use of capital letters is so inconsistent, it's distracting.

- I need to clean up the piece considerably in terms of grammar and usage.

1 GETTING STARTED

Presentation

the physical appearance of the piece—the welcome mat that invites the reader in

6 EXPERT

HIGH

My piece's appearance makes it easy to read and enjoy. I've taken care to ensure that it is pleasing to my reader's eye.

- I've written clearly and legibly. My letters, words, and the spaces between them are uniform.
- My choice of font style, size, and/or color makes my piece a breeze to read.
- My margins frame the text nicely. There are no tears, smudges, or cross-outs.
- Text features such as bulleted lists, charts, pictures, and headers are working well.

5 WELL DONE

4 ALMOST THERE

MIDDLE

My piece still looks like a draft. Many visual elements should be cleaned up and handled with more care.

- My handwriting is readable, but my letters and words and the spaces between them should be treated more consistently.
- My choice of font style, size, and/or color seems "off"—inappropriate for my intended audience.
- My margins are uneven. There are some tears, smudges, or cross-outs.
- I've handled simple text features well but am struggling with the more complex ones.

3 MAKING STRIDES

2 ON MY WAY

LOW

My piece is almost unreadable because of its appearance. It's not ready for anyone but me to read.

- My handwriting is so hard to read, it creates a visual barrier.
- The font styles, sizes, and/or colors I've chosen are dizzying. They're not working.
- My margins are uneven or nonexistent, making the piece difficult to read.
- I haven't used text features well, even simple ones.

1 GETTING STARTED

Common Prefixes and Suffixes

Prefixes A prefix is a letter or group of letters added to the beginning of a root to change its meaning.

Prefix	Definition	Prefix	Definition
acro-	high, topmost, at the extremity	**mis-**	bad, badly, wrongly
ambi-, amphi-	both, around, about	**mono-**	one, alone, single
anti-	against, opposed to	**multi-**	many
auto-	self	**neo-**	new, young, recent, latest
bi-	two, twice, on two sides	**non-**	not, lacking, without
by-	near, side, secondary or incidental	**ob-, oc-, of-**	before, against, over
co-, col-, com-, con-, cor-	together with, joint, to the same degree	**oct-, octa-, octo-**	eight
		over-	upper, outer, superior, passing above, too much
de-	from, down, reverse the action	**paleo-**	ancient, early
deca-	ten	**pan-**	all, every, universal
deci-	one-tenth	**para-**	at the side of, in a secondary position
di-	two, double, twice; not, away from (see *dis-*)	**penta-**	five
dia-	through, throughout, apart, between	**per-**	through, throughout, completely, very thoroughly
dis-	not, opposite of, lack of, away from	**peri-**	around, about, enclosing, near
e-	out, beyond, away from, without	**poly-**	many, much, excessive
em-, en-	put into or on, cover, make, subject to	**post-**	after, later
endo-	within	**pre-**	before, in front of, superior to
epi-	upon, over, on the outside	**pro-**	for, forward
equa-, equi-	equal, equally	**proto-**	first
ex- (w/hyphen)	former	**pseudo-**	false, deceptive
ex-	out of, outside, from	**quad-**	four
fore-	before, ahead of, front	**quint-**	five
hemi-	half	**re-**	again, back, reverse
hetero-	different	**self-**	by oneself, within, automatic
hex-, hexa-	six	**sest-, sex-**	six
homo-	same, equal to, like	**sub-**	under, beneath, to a lesser degree, bordering
il-, im-, in-, ir-	not, lack of	**super-, supr-**	above, beyond, over
im-, in-	in, into, within	**syl-, sym-, syn-, sys-**	with, together
inter-	between	**tele-**	at, over, or from a distance, far away
intra-	within, inside	**tetra-**	four
macr-, macro-	large, long	**trans-**	across, beyond, over
mal-	bad, badly, wrong, ill	**tri-**	three
mega-	very large, great, powerful	**un-**	not, the opposite of
meta-	change in, after, going beyond or higher	**under-**	beneath, below normal, too little
micro-	very small, minute	**uni-**	one, only
mid-	middle		
mini-	small, brief		

Common Prefixes and Suffixes (continued)

Suffixes A suffix is a letter or group of letters added to the end of a root to form a new word. Adding a suffix often requires a spelling change to the root word.

Suffix	Definition	Suffix	Definition
-able, -ible	capable of, likely to, worthy of	-ish	having the characteristics of, native to
-al, -ial	of, related to, having the characteristics of	-ism	act of, state of, school of, system, manner
-ance, -ancy	state of, quality of, act of, process of	-ist	a person who, that which
-ant, -ent	someone who, agent of, performing the task of	-itis	disease, inflammation of, preoccupation with
-ar, -er, -or	someone who, something that, native of	-ity, -ty	state of, quality of being, instance of
-ary, -ory	relating to, having the qualities of, place where	-ive, -ative, -itive	causing, tending to do something
-asis, -esis, -osis	action, condition, process	-ize	make, cause to become, subject to, engage in
-ate	cause, make, provide or treat with	-less	without, not able to be
-cian, -ian	a person who practices or performs a skill	-like	similar to, resembling
-cide	kill, killing, killer	-ly	in the manner of, in the order of
-cy	action, function, rank, condition of being	-mania	exaggerated enthusiasm, uncontrollable desire
-dom	quality of, state of, realm of, power of		
-ee	one who is receiving or performing an action	-ment	action of, process of, result of, degree of being
-en	made of, added to	-meter	measure; device for measuring
-ence, -ency	state of, quality	-ness	state of, quality of
-er	more than (compares two things); one that is or engages in some activity or profession	-ology, -logy	study of, science of, branch of learning
		-or	one that does a specific thing
-ery	place to or for, practice of, product of, condition of	-ous, -eous, -ious	full of, having the qualities of
-ese	native of, language of	-phobia	fear, hatred
-est	most (compares three or more things)	-scope	an instrument for seeing
-ful	full of, having the quality of, able to cause	-ship	condition of, state of, quality of being, skill of
-fy	make	-tude	state of, condition of, instance of being
-hood	place, time, period, state of, quality of, group of	-ure	state of being, process of, condition of, result of
-ic	having the characteristics of, causing	-ward	in the direction of
-ice	condition of, state of	-y	characterized by, inclined to, tending to
-ile	related to, capable of, suitable for		
-ion, -sion, -tion, -ation	act of, state of, process of		